PRAISE FOR *VEGANOMICS*

"Cooney's book is filled with hard science and fascinating insights, but most of all it builds a firm foundation from which the vegan movement can chart its course."

—**Kathy Freston**, *New York Times* Bestselling Author of
Quantum Wellness and *The Lean*

"*Veganomics* offers a fascinating look at the rise of vegetarianism, as well as intriguing insight into the hearts and minds of the compassionate people who choose to leave meat off their plates. You will be captivated and informed, but most importantly, inspired." —**Nathan Runkle**, Executive Director, Mercy For Animals

"When it comes to animal protection work, it's not enough just to be right: animals need us to be both right and effective. Nick Cooney's combed through the scientific literature on what's effective (and what's not) so you don't have to. For the sake of animals, read it now!"

—**Paul Shapiro**, Vice President of Farm Animal Protection,
The Humane Society of the United States

"A must-read for anyone who is serious about making the world a kinder place for animals." —**Gene Baur**, Co-Founder and President, Farm Sanctuary

"*Veganomics* is among the most important, practical, well-researched, and interesting books to grace the animal advocacy arena in a long time. Cooney's effortless prose makes digesting so much rich information into a delicious reading experience. Cooney has taken the movement to the next level, from the what to the how, and perhaps just in time." —**Jeff Lydon**, Executive Director, VegFund

"Nick Cooney is helping revolutionize vegan advocacy by shining a spotlight on the need for research to measure results. It's a must-read for anyone who cares about creating more vegans and helping farmed animals."

—**Che Green**, Executive Director, Humane Research Council

"*Veganomics* is one of the most useful and important books on vegetarian advocacy written to date. If you're looking to be a more effective vegetarian advocate, this book is essential."

—**Jon Camp**, Director of Outreach, Vegan Outreach

"Casting aside philosophy and moralizing, Cooney sifts through the data with a steely-eyed pragmatism towards what works and what doesn't in promoting a cruelty-free diet."

—**Bruce Friedrich**, Co-Author of *The Animal Activist's Handbook*

"*Veganomics* is a meticulously researched book with major implications for anyone who enjoys meat-free meals. Cooney is the Nate Silver of the vegetarian world, crunching the numbers in an entertaining and engaging way to uncover surprising truths about our diets and ourselves."

—**Michael Greger**, M.D., Founder, NutritionFacts.org

"Whether you are an animal advocate yourself, or just want to understand the culture, Cooney provides answers to the questions you didn't know you had. Read it, get informed, and make a difference."

—**Jon Bockman**, Executive Director, EffectiveAnimalActivism.org

"With *Veganomics*, Nick Cooney firmly establishes himself as a fresh voice with novel perspectives on the *hows* and *whys* of reaching ever-larger numbers with the plant-based message. It's also a fun book, with interesting, memorable factoids on every page that you will search for opportunities to work into conversation at the water cooler or your next party."

—**Joseph Connelly**, Founder and Publisher, *VegNews* magazine

"*Veganomics* is a must-read for anyone who intends to take research-based vegan advocacy to the next level. You won't agree with everything he writes—and that's exactly what makes it so powerful. Cooney's challenge to our movement is to put aside our biases in order to bring our 'A' game for farmed animals."

—**Michael A. Webermann**, Executive Director,
Farm Animal Rights Movement (FARM)

"Supremely readable and thought provoking, this book sheds new light on what it is going to take for more Americans to give up turkey for Tofurky® and other meat alternatives. Marketers of vegan foods would pay thousands of dollars for this level of information and not learn as much."

—**Seth Tibbott**, Founder and President, The Tofurky® Company

"A great book the vegan movement has been waiting for for decades. *Veganomics* is surely the most complete compendium on vegetarians and vegans."

—**Sebastian Zösch**, CEO, German Vegetarian Association (VEBU)

"If you want to help more animals by spreading veg eating, *Veganomics* is a must-read. Nick Cooney has given us a powerful resource that can dramatically accelerate the progress of the veg movement." —**Caryn Ginsberg**, Author of *Animal Impact*

"Blending demographics and social psychology, Cooney's sharp analysis will provide a wealth of support for the already converted. More importantly, it will make the prospect of joining this impressive and growing cohort of the population irresistible for anyone who thinks seriously about the powerful connection between food and identity." —**James McWilliams**, Author of *Just Food* and *The Politics of the Pasture*

"Nick Cooney states in his book that, as activists, we should be asking ourselves 'How can I do the most possible good in the world?' Well, the answer as to how we invest our time more effectively begins with reading *Veganomics*. This book is absolutely essential for anyone who cares about animals and wants to make a difference. It is an enormous contribution to the animal rights movement."

—**Sharon Núñez**, Co-Founder, Animal Equality

"It's about time we go from guessing to knowing what's best for the animals. This book is an important milestone on this path. Nick Cooney's work has proven to be invaluable for the animal protection movement."

—**Mahi Klosterhalfen**, CEO and president, Albert Schweitzer Foundation for Our Contemporaries

"Based on scientific data and enriched with vivid reflections, Cooney encourages all animal advocates to maintain ambitious but realistic goals to build a more compassionate world."

—**Daniela Romero Waldhorn**, General Director, AnimaNaturalis International

VEGANOMICS

THE SURPRISING SCIENCE ON
VEGETARIANS,
FROM THE BREAKFAST TABLE
TO THE BEDROOM

NICK COONEY

Lantern Books ● New York
A Division of Booklight Inc.

2014
Lantern Books
128 Second Place
Brooklyn, NY 11231
www.lanternbooks.com

Library of Congress Cataloging-in-Publication Data

Cooney, Nick.
Veganomics : the surprising science on vegetarians, from the breakfast table to the bedroom /
Nick Cooney.
pages cm
Includes bibliographical references.
ISBN 978-1-59056-428-8 (pbk. : alk. paper)—ISBN 978-1-59056-429-5 (ebook)
1. Vegetarianism. 2. Vegetarians. I. Title.
TX392.C697 2013
641.5'636—dc23
2013029884

CONTENTS

INTRODUCTION

FLIP THROUGH A MAGAZINE, BROWSE ONLINE, OR TURN ON the television, and it quickly becomes clear: vegetarian eating is on the rise. Bookstores devote whole aisles to vegetarian cookbooks. Columnists like the *New York Times'* Mark Bittman are singing the praises of meat-free meals. Entire school districts in Baltimore, Los Angeles, and elsewhere are removing meat from their menus every Monday.

Average meat consumption in the U.S. dropped nearly 10 percent between 2006 and 2012. Part of the decline was caused by the growing number of vegetarians and vegans. Meat reducers—people eating less meat to improve their health or for other reasons—also played a major role. While the lowering of meat consumption was specific to the U.S., vegetarian eating has also become more common in Canada, Australia, and across Europe over the past two decades.

Just who are vegetarians, and why are their numbers growing? Although vegetarians aren't all the same, real differences exist between them as a group and their omnivorous counterparts. They differ not only in eating habits and ethics, but also in their psychology, perceptions about the world, personalities, friendship choices, and even their sex lives.

This is a book about vegetarians. It's about who they are and why they are. If you're a vegetarian, vegan, semi-vegetarian, or any other veg-affiliated person, get ready to learn a lot more about your kind and what makes you different from—and similar to—your meat-eating brethren. And get ready to feel even better about your choice to leave animal products off your plate.

Although I hope this book will be an interesting and entertaining read, I want advocates of vegetarian eating to use it for a more serious purpose: to be more effective at getting others to ditch meat.

For each person who adopts a compassionate diet, dozens of intelligent, unique animals will be spared a lifetime of misery. With the cultural tide shifting away from meat, and vegetarian options becoming more common at restaurants and grocery stores, it is now easier than ever for people to cut cruelty from their diet.

But that doesn't mean that getting them to do so is simple.

To be as effective as possible, advocates of vegetarian eating need to better understand human psychology and what does and does not work in inspiring people to change. I wrote about this at length in my previous book, *Change of Heart: What Psychology Can Teach Us About Spreading Social Change* (Cooney 2011). But advocates also need to understand a lot more about vegetarians themselves. Why do some people give up meat, and what prevents others from doing the same? How do people transition from being a meat-eater to being a vegetarian, and are there ways to make that process easier? What types of people are most likely to go vegetarian? And why do so many vegetarians eventually go back to eating meat?

This book answers these questions and many more like them—not with predictions, anecdotal evidence, or interviews with so-called experts, but with valid scientific research. Tucked away in arcane academic journals like *Family Economics and Nutrition Review* and *Social Psychological and Personality Science* are hundreds of peer-reviewed studies on these very topics. Most of these studies were carried out in the United States or Europe, though some come from Canada, Australia, or elsewhere around the globe. Many of their findings are completely unknown—and incredibly useful—to those who want to promote vegetarian eating.

Some of the studies can also be pretty entertaining. For example, there was the experiment on whether vegetarians smell better than meat-eaters, and the study that put vegetarians and meat-eaters in fMRI machines to see which group really had the more compassionate brains. There was also the survey that asked whether vegetarians or meat-eaters were more giving in the bedroom.

All these questions and more will be answered on the following pages. But be forewarned: you may never look at vegetarians the same way again.

1

MOVE ASIDE, COWS AND PIGS

HOW WHAT WE EAT REALLY IMPACTS ANIMALS

DOES BEING VEGETARIAN REALLY HELP ANIMALS? IT SOUNDS silly to some, but to many people it's a serious question. One study discovered that fewer than half of all meat-eaters think going vegetarian prevents cruelty to farm animals (Lea, Moving from Meat). Scroll through the comments on any YouTube video on factory farming and you'll see that same sentiment over and over: "This is bad, but going vegetarian won't help, the animals will still be treated that way."

So does being a vegetarian really help animals? And if so, how many animals—and what kinds of animals—does it help? Not only are the answers surprising, they also have major implications for anyone who wants to promote vegetarian eating.

By the way, in this book we'll use the phrase "vegetarian eating" and not "vegan eating" for two reasons. First, nearly every study we refer to focuses on vegetarians. The results might apply to vegans, and to promoting vegan eating, but we can't assume that. It also would be impractical to use the phrase "vegetarians and vegans" in every sentence. "Vegetarians" is a simpler term and it covers both vegetarians and vegans. As you'll see though, our hope is the public will cut all cruelty out of their diet—including eggs and dairy.

HOW MANY ANIMALS DOES A VEGETARIAN SPARE?

How many farm animals are killed each year for the average American omnivore? Dr. Harish Sethu at the blog CountingAnimals.com analyzed data from the U.S. Department of Agriculture to find out. As of 2012, about 31 farm animals suffer and die for the average meat-eater. In rounded figures, the number of animals killed breaks down to:

28 chickens
1 turkey
½ pig
⅛ beef cow
1⅓ farm-raised fish
  (Sethu, How Many Animals)

The consumption of dairy and eggs adds about two more animals into the mix:

2 chickens (one laying hen, one male chick that is killed shortly after birth)
$\frac{1}{30}$ dairy cow
  (Norwood and Lusk)

If we consider shellfish and wild fish, the numbers grow dramatically higher:

Over 225 fish
Over 151 shellfish
  (Sethu, How Many Animals)

Most of the shellfish—such as shrimp, crabs, lobsters, and squids—are eaten directly. Some wild fish are consumed in the same way, but many are fed to farm-raised fish to help fatten them up. If those numbers of fish seem high to you, keep in mind that many fish—such as anchovies—are very small.

As you may have noticed, we've left out animals that are eaten in relatively small numbers, such as goats, rabbits, and sheep. We're also ignoring the indirect ways that animals are killed in the meat production process. For example, we're not including the fish and other wild animals killed when pollution from factory farms seeps into waterways. We're also not including the wild animals who are killed by pesticide poisoning, or who are run over by farm threshing equipment, on corn and soy fields. (Vegetarians are responsible for some of these deaths as well, but not to the same degree as meat-eaters. Producing meat requires a lot of grain.)

Looking at the number of animals killed for food, we see a surprising picture. When most people think about food animals, they envision a cow. But far more fish are killed for food than any other type of animal. And when it comes to farm animal deaths, chickens easily rule the roost.

For every cow they eat, Americans eat 190 chickens and kill over 1,400 fish. For every pig they eat, Americans eat 60 chickens and kill over 450 fish.

The disparity is even larger when we look at specific animal products. In their entire adult life the average American omnivore will cause the death of only about two dairy cows, eight beef cows, and 30 pigs. But they'll kill about 80 farm-raised fish, 120 egg industry hens, and a whopping 1,680 broiler chickens. If you can bear to see the astronomical numbers for wild fish and shellfish, here they are: over their entire adult life, the average American meat-eater is responsible for the killing of over 13,500 wild fish and 9,060 shellfish.

CALCULATING CRUELTY

Just what do these numbers mean for those who want to promote vegetarian eating? If vegetarian advocates want as many individuals as possible to be protected from cruelty, an important lesson is: focus on getting the public to give up chicken, fish, and eggs.

Cutting out red meat is a valuable goal, but if that is all a person does they will spare less than one animal per year. If they replace that red meat with chicken or fish, they will actually be harming many more animals.

On the other hand, by simply eating half as much chicken flesh as they used to a person can spare 14 farm animals per year. A person who gives up eating chickens entirely—even if they replace all of the chicken they used to eat with beef and pork—will spare 27 to 28 animals. If the entire country did that, the number of farm animals killed each year in the U.S. would drop from about 8.5 billion to 1 billion—even though Americans will be eating as much meat as they did before.

Eating fish appears to kill an even larger number of animals. As we saw earlier, about 225 wild fish are killed each year for the average meat-eater's consumption. But a person who stops eating fish doesn't actually prevent 225 fish from being killed. Why? Because most fish are omnivores—they eat other, smaller fish. So if humans did not eat a wild-caught tuna fish, that animal would be eating hundreds of other fish.

As a result, we don't know the number of wild animals impacted when a person stops eating fish.

The number of animals' deaths we're responsible for might not be what's most important to vegetarian advocates. Perhaps the main concern should not be the number, but the amount of suffering that's caused. In that case, priorities shift. Vegetarian advocates need to consider not just the number of animals killed but also how badly each animal suffers, and how long that suffering goes on for.

If reducing animal suffering is the main concern, then considerations about fish become less important. For most wild fish, the point of slaughter is the only time at which humans impact their existence. Most farm animals, on the other hand, endure a lifetime of misery. They are strictly confined on factory farms, and selective breeding causes them painful physical problems. Only farm-raised fish suffer to the same degree. Shellfish also take a back seat when we focus on the suffering of animals. Like fish, most shellfish come from the wild and their death similarly is the only occasion we affect their lives. And some shellfish, such as oysters and clams, are species that *may* not feel pain.

We can calculate the number of days each farm-animal species suffers because of the average meat-eater's diet. For example, since the average American eats half of a pig each year, and a pig lives for 180 days before being slaughtered, the average pork consumer causes 90 days of pig suffering per year.

How do animal products stack up against one another when measured this way?

In terms of days spent suffering per year, the average meat-eater generates about 1,100 days of misery for chickens, an entire year for egg-laying hens, 120 days for turkeys, 90 days for pigs, 23 days for beef cows, and 12 days for dairy cows. Depending on what species of fish they eat, the average American also causes between 355 and 2,470 days of farmed-fish suffering each year (Farm Animal Welfare).

But we can't just stop there. We still have to factor in how *severely* each animal suffers. For example, it is likely that an egg-laying hen experiences a lot more agony than a cow raised for beef. Egg-laying hens are kept for their entire lives in dirty wire cages so small they can barely turn around. Beef cows typically spend most of their time roaming open pastures. They aren't intensely confined until the last few weeks or months of their life.

We don't know exactly to what extent each species of farm animal experiences pain and misery, but animal welfare studies shed light on which ones probably undergo the most wretched existences. In his book *Compassion, by the Pound,* co-written with his fellow agricultural economist Jayson Lusk, F. Bailey Norwood reviews some of that research and shares his perceptions of how much farm animals suffer. On a scale of -10 to 10, with 10 being the most pleasant conditions, he rates the welfare of farm animals as follows:

Beef cows: 6
Dairy cows: 4
Broiler (meat) chickens: 3
Pigs: −2
Egg-laying hens: −8
    (Norwood and Lusk)

For another perspective, we turn to Dr. Sara Shields. Dr. Shields is an animal welfare expert who, along with a team of others, researches and writes the Humane Society of the United States' rigorous white papers on farm animal welfare. On the same -10 to 10 scale, Dr. Shields rates the welfare of farm animals as follows:

Beef cows: 2
Dairy cows: 0
Pigs: −5
Fish: −7
Egg-laying hens: −7
Broiler (meat) chickens and turkeys: −8
    (Shields)

Although Shields' ratings are lower, both she and Norwood follow roughly the same pattern. The only substantial difference is for broiler chickens and turkeys, which Shields rates as having the most wretched lives of all farm animals.

Averaging Shields' and Norwood's scores together, we can assume that egg-laying hens and farm-raised fish probably endure the most suffering. When we consider how these animals are raised, it's easy to see why. Egg-laying hens experience more than just very cramped cages. Their beaks are often partly seared off with a laser, and many hens lose their feathers from constantly rubbing against the bars of their cages. Their feet become crippled from standing on wire-mesh flooring their whole life.

Farm-raised fish are penned in densely packed, waste-filled pools. Up to a third of them die slowly from disease or parasites. Some have their face or flesh chewed off by sea lice. Because the close confinement increases aggression, some fishes' fins, tails, or eyes are bitten off and out by other fish.

Pigs and chickens raised for meat follow next on the scale of affliction. Both species are crammed into indoor pens or sheds with little room to move around. Sows are enclosed for most of their lives in cages so small they cannot turn around. Many meat-chickens (known as broilers) experience crippling leg disorders, heart attacks, and other painful ailments as a result of being bred to grow so large, so quickly. Hundreds of millions of them expire on the floors of their sheds, not even making it to the slaughterhouse.

Both Norwood and Shields agree that cows used by the dairy and beef industries endure the least painful lives. Even though they are abused in many ways, overall, cows undergo far less torment than chickens, farm-raised fish, and pigs.

Having considered how grievously each type of farm animal suffers, how many of them do so, and for how long, one thing becomes clear: vegetarian advocates should focus on getting the public to cut out chicken, farm-raised fish, and eggs.

When we look at the *days* of suffering that farm animals bear for the average meat-eater, there's no contest. Chickens and fish account for 92 percent of those days of suffering. Turkeys make up a modest 4 percent, and pigs a mere 3 percent. Cows, both beef and dairy combined, make up just 1 percent of the number.

If we look at the total *number* of farm animals raised and killed, the proportions are almost identical. Chickens and fish account for 95 percent of farm animals butchered. Turkeys make up just 3 percent, pigs are 1.5 percent, and cows represent just 0.5 percent of all animals killed.

The simple truth is that chickens and farm-raised fish probably lead the most miserable lives of any farm animal. To the extent that promoting vegetarianism means encouraging a diet that is kind toward animals, one can argue that virtually all that matters is getting the public to cut out or cut back on eating chickens, farm-raised fish, and eggs. Nearly all of the good that a vegan or vegetarian does for farm animals comes from removing chicken, farm-raised fish, and eggs from their diet. Pork and turkey represent only small slices of the pie of suffering. Beef and dairy are statistically almost insignificant. This holds true both for the amount of misery cows undergo, how long they endure it for, and the numbers of animals that are affected.

DOES THIS FEEL WEIRD TO YOU?

Looking at our diet and farm animals in this way might feel odd. It might appear as if we're seeing animals as mere numbers instead of individuals. Advocates of vegetarian eating might even believe it betrays those animals who aren't "important" enough to focus on (specifically cows and pigs, but also ducks, geese, goats, sheep, and rabbits). It's also difficult for any of us *not* to focus on pigs and cows since we tend to see them as more intelligent and human-like than chickens and fish.

If all of this feels weird to you, it's because human beings don't usually make ethical decisions based on calculations. For example, when people were asked in one study how much they'd pay to improve the welfare of an individual egg-laying hen, they replied that they'd pay about a dollar. When they were asked how much they would pay to improve the welfare of a hundred hens, they responded that they'd pay about $15—or just 15 cents a bird. To improve the lives of the nearly 300 million egg laying hens in the U.S., people indicated they'd be willing to lay out a paltry $340—which comes out to about one ten-thousandth of a cent per animal. (A third of respondents said they wouldn't pay a penny.) Furthermore, even though pigs and egg-laying hens are intelligent and unique individuals, people in this study were willing to pay about three times more money to improve the lives of pigs than they were to better the lives of hens (Norwood and Lusk).

On the outside looking in, it's easy to judge the people surveyed as possessing a very muddled ethical sense. Logically, if improving the life of one chicken is worth spending one dollar on, then enhancing the lives of a hundred chickens should be worth spending $100 on. Sure, a few people might not be able to spare $100, but most could. And for those of us who see all animals as having more or less equal value, it's easy to criticize those who would pay $3 to help a pig but only $1 to help a chicken.

The fact is that using logic in this manner is simply not how the human mind works. Our beliefs and ethics don't come from a thoughtful computation on how we can do the most good. They should, but they don't. Unfortunately, our empathy often seems to be split from our calculating, analytical minds. Even thinking with the analytical part of our brains seems to make us less compassionate (Cooney 2011). This isn't only true when it comes to animals; it's the case for most social issues.

If our ethical choices were based on logic and we heard that millions of people were starving in Africa we'd give more money to help those millions than if we heard about one, undernourished child. Yet studies show the opposite is true: focusing on how large a problem is causes us to donate less (Cooney 2011).

In the same vein, all of us would agree that saving a child from dying of easily preventable malaria is more important than supporting the performance of a local orchestra. Yet Americans contribute dramatically more to the arts each year than they do to efforts to eradicate malaria (Giving USA 2012).

For most people, the goal of any altruistic act is simply to do something helpful. Very few of us choose where to donate, where to volunteer, and how to live our lives based on the answer to the question, "How can I do the most possible good in the world?" And yet it is that calculating attitude that is crucial to helping as many animals (or people) as possible.

Some nonprofits are starting to catch on. For example, the Bill & Melinda Gates Foundation focuses on issues where they can save the greatest number of human lives per dollar. This orientation includes very successful efforts to decrease the instances of malaria, to vaccinate more children, and to improve child health in poorer nations. The Foundation constantly gathers data to determine how many lives it is saving, and what it can do to save even more for the same amount of money (Bill and Melinda Gates Foundation).

Does such an approach mean the Foundation is turning its back on those who suffer in other ways around the globe? Not at all. The Gateses see value in every human life, but they know their resources are limited and try to put them toward programs that will save the most lives. Literally millions of children are only alive today because the Gates Foundation chose to take this analytical approach to improving the world. If the Foundation had spent an equal amount of money on improving the world and had been equally passionate about its work, but had not taken a data-based approach, most of those children would be dead.

Using a similar method in its philanthropy, the website GiveWell.org reviews hundreds of charities and provides recommendations to donors about which organizations will save the most lives per dollar donated. The website

EffectiveAnimalActivism.org was launched in 2012 to provide similar advice for donors wanting to support animal protection causes.

PUTTING IT INTO PRACTICE

Advocates of vegetarian eating can and should take a page from the strategy of GiveWell, the Bill & Melinda Gates Foundation, and other charities that are moving toward data-based altruism. By doing so, they can spare many, many more animals from a lifetime of suffering.

One way to accomplish this is to focus on the foods where, as we've seen, activists can get the most bang for their buck, as it were: chicken, fish, and eggs. Concentrating on these three products, especially chicken, could mean the difference between helping hundreds of animals and helping thousands.

Many vegetarian advocates are already doing this. In conversations with friends or the public, they make sure to emphasize that nearly all of the farm animals killed for food are chickens. They point out that by simply cutting out or cutting back on eating chicken, each of us can spare dozens of animals a year from a lifetime of misery. When talking with people who are considering changing their diet, they encourage them to cut out chicken as the first step. They may also point out the possible health risks of eating chicken and fish, while intentionally not mentioning the health risks of red meat.

And it's not just individual advocates who are adopting this new strategy. Surveys conducted by vegetarian advocacy groups such as Farm Animal Rights Movement, The Humane League, and Farm Sanctuary suggest that placing extra and explicit emphasis on chicken in their outreach efforts worked. It led to more animals being spared a wretched existence and death.

THE IDEAL MESSAGE

If vegetarian advocates aim to promote the dietary changes that will spare the greatest number of animals, they need to consider something else. The public may be much more willing to give up certain products than they are to give up animal products entirely.

Leaving aside the issue of chicken for a moment, consider the difference between encouraging someone to go vegetarian and urging that person to go vegan. Vegetarians do almost as much good for farm animals as vegans. They reduce 88 percent as many days of suffering, and spare 94 percent as many lives. And if you're talking about vegetarians who give up eggs, by both measures they do over 99 percent as much good.

Unfortunately, many vegans forget this fact. They fixate on the negative aspects of vegetarian eating instead of considering the positives. One study suggested that the most common belief vegans held about vegetarians was not that the latter were helping animals or eating more healthily, but that they were hypocrites (Povey *et al.* 2001). Talk about missing the forest for the trees!

Although vegans do only slightly more good for farm animals than vegetarians, meat-eaters perceive a vegan diet as much more unrealistic. A 2001 study from the U.K. found that although meat-eaters had mixed feelings about vegetarianism, a number of them perceived the diet as healthier, along with other benefits. On the other hand, meat-eaters saw veganism as unhealthful, extreme, and restrictive; not one had anything positive to say about being a vegan. Even many pescatarians and vegetarians have the perception that veganism is difficult and potentially not healthy (Povey *et al.* 2001).

Meat-eaters probably have a better impression of veganism today than they did more than a decade ago. But in all likelihood, they continue to think of vegetarian eating as a healthier and more viable lifestyle than veganism. They also continue to like vegetarians more than they do vegans (Americans Pick Ronald McDonald). As a result, nearly everyone who wants a more animal-friendly diet starts off by going vegetarian, pescatarian, or semi-vegetarian. Even the vast majority of vegans spent several years as vegetarians before taking the next step (Hirschler 2011).

Communication researchers have found that to get people to alter their behavior most significantly, advocates should promote a change that is substantial but that individuals can picture themselves accomplishing (Cooney 2011). Clearly, most meat-eaters cannot and would not want to picture themselves as vegans. As we've seen, they think that veganism is unhealthful, restrictive, and extreme. But a number of meat-eaters *could* picture themselves as vegetarians. One study suggested that a full 7 percent of American meat-eaters could be willing to give up meat entirely (Humane Research Council, Advocating Meat Reduction).

When you add to this the fact that vegans spare only slightly more animals than vegetarians, the implication becomes clear. By encouraging people to go vegetarian, you should lead to more animals being spared than encouraging them to go vegan. A "go vegetarian" message should also lead to the most vegans in the long term, since once a person becomes a vegetarian they're more likely to go vegan than if they're encouraged to move from omnivorism to veganism (Stahler, Retention Survey).

This observation hasn't been proven yet. It's an assumption based on general research about communication, persuasion, and perceptions of vegetarianism and veganism. We might hope that research will be done soon to confirm this is the case.

The logic applied above also brings us back to chickens. Animal advocates may be able to spare more animals by encouraging the public to avoid eating chicken—or by encouraging them to avoid eating chicken, fish, and eggs—than by urging them to go vegetarian. Why might this be the case?

Try this scenario: Imagine it's ten years in the future. Climate change remains a major issue and the time has come for you to buy a new car. An environmentalist friend encourages you to just stop driving entirely. Another friend presses you to buy a solar-powered car, which generates 90 percent fewer greenhouse gases, is equally convenient, and is almost as cheap as a conventional car. What would you do?

While a few people may quit driving entirely, many more would be willing to buy the solar car. And in making the switch, they'd be doing 90 percent as much good for the environment as if they had stopped driving entirely. It is the second message—the one encouraging people to buy a solar-powered car—that would be a more effective one for protecting the Earth. Persuading five people to buy the solar car would do more to lower greenhouse-gas emissions than getting four people to stop driving entirely.

The same situation holds true when it comes to the meat Americans eat. Simply by ditching chicken—even if they replace it with beef and pork—Americans can reduce the number of farm animals they are killing by about 90 percent. True, if they replaced all of that chicken with farm-raised fish and eggs, the switch would be of little to no benefit for animals. But it seems unlikely that many people would do that. In all likelihood, the public would be more willing to give up one type of meat than to give up all meat. Indeed, polls show that there are far more chicken-avoiders than vegetarians. One national poll found that while only two percent of Americans were vegetarian at that time, 6 percent said they did not eat chicken. (It's also worth noting that 9 percent said they did not eat eggs, and 15 percent stated they did not eat fish.) (Stahler, How Many Adults)

Focusing on chicken could prove more beneficial in the long run as well. People who eliminate one food become more open to other changes later on, and they've already taken the most important step by no longer eating chicken. To the extent they spread this behavioral change to friends and family members, they're leading to an alteration in their diet that spares 90 percent of farm animals and is much easier to adopt than vegetarianism.

Only research will be able to tell us for sure whether encouraging people to "go vegan," "go vegetarian," "cut back on meat," or "ditch chicken" helps the most animals. Vegetarian advocates may find, though, that encouraging people to simply cut out or cut back on chicken (or chicken, eggs, and fish) spares more animals in both the short and long term.

BUT WAIT, DO VEGETARIANS REALLY SPARE ALL THOSE ANIMALS?

This is all very interesting, you may say, but have we really answered the question that kicked off this chapter? How do we know that going vegetarian actually spares real, live animals from a life of suffering? And is there anything we're missing in calculating how many animals a vegetarian spares?

In a general sense, it's clear that when a portion of the public goes vegetarian or eats less meat the number of animals killed for food drops. Like every other product, meat is subject to the laws of supply and demand. As demand for a product goes down, producers start making less of it. Americans were eating about 10 percent less meat per person in 2012 than they were in 2006. As a result in 2012 there were hundreds of millions of animals who were not bred, raised in cruel factory-farm conditions, and killed at a slaughterhouse.

But there's another rule of supply and demand that we've been ignoring. When demand for a product goes down, the unwanted product ends up sitting on the shelf. Producers and retailers want to sell it, but there aren't enough customers willing to buy it. So what do retailers do? They lower the price. So when demand goes down, the price falls as well. And the lower prices in turn drive demand slightly back up.

What does this mean for vegetarians? If you decide to leave 50 pounds of chicken off your plate this year, that doesn't mean that 50 fewer pounds will be produced next year. The amount of chicken that won't be produced is something less than 50 pounds. Norwood and Lusk have calculated what the actual impact is when someone—such as a vegetarian—decides to leave animal products off their plate. Their model predicts the following:

- If you give up one pound of beef, total beef production eventually falls by .68 pounds
- If you give up one pound of chicken, total chicken production eventually falls by .76 pounds
- If you give up one pound of pork, total pork production eventually falls by .74 pounds
- If you give up one pound of milk, total milk production eventually falls by .56 pounds
- If you give up one pound of eggs, total egg production eventually falls by .91 pounds

(Norwood and Lusk)

In other words, leaving animal products off of our plates doesn't do quite as much good as we thought. While it's true that the average American omnivore kills 33 farm animals each year, going vegan will only spare about 25 animals per year. Going vegetarian will spare 23 animals.

This seems like bad news. However, there's a big upside. The same rates hold true when people add more meat to their diet, or when new meat-eaters are born. If your neighbor decides to eat a hundred extra pounds of chicken this year, total chicken production will only increase by 76 pounds.

Of course, at the individual level this is all a bit silly. Norwood and Lusk have calculated down to the per-pound level what is really a large-scale phenomenon. If Americans eat ten thousand fewer pounds of chicken this year, farmers will take notice. Next year, they'll produce about 7,600 fewer pounds of chicken meat. If only one person eats less chicken, the industry is not going to notice.

In that sense, eating is like donating to charity. Let's say that one particular non-profit spends in all about $20 for each child they vaccinate against a deadly disease. Does that mean that if you donate $20 you can be sure that one additional child will be vaccinated? No. The charity is not going to cash your check, smile, and then go find one more kid to vaccinate with your $20. So should you still donate? Of course! Because the principle works, except on a larger scale. If a thousand people each donate $20, then most likely a thousand additional children will be vaccinated. That

$20,000, when pooled together, would be enough to open another clinic in a new village.

The same holds true for avoiding animal products. If you decide to stop eating meat, will the chicken farmer near you actually raise and kill 28 (or rather 22, once you factor in supply-and-demand fluctuations) fewer chickens next year? No. But as soon as some modest number of people have decided to go vegetarian, their collective impact will be noticed. The farmer will cut back on production, at a rate of about 22 chickens per new vegetarian.

As researcher Jason Gaverick Matheny has pointed out, each person who gives up meat has a chance of being the one who tips the scales. Each new vegetarian could be the person who brings the total quantity of meat being boycotted to a large enough level that farmers take notice and reduce the number of animals they raise (Matheny 2002).

For example, let's say chicken farmers only notice and adjust production levels once a thousand people have ditched chicken. At that point, farmers would decrease production by 22,000 birds. Chances are small that your decision not to eat meat would be the one that brought the total amount of chicken being boycotted to that threshold. In fact, your chances would be only one in a thousand. But if you were that lucky person, your decision would spare 22,000 chickens! In other words, by giving up chicken, you'd have a one-in-a-thousand chance of sparing 22,000 animals.

Clearly, the ethical thing to do is to stop eating chickens. This is true even if you can't be sure that your individual choice will be the one that tips the scales. But when you average it out among all of the vegetarians across the country, each of you would have spared 22 chickens from a lifetime of misery.

So congratulations vegetarians, vegans, and meat reducers—you really are making a difference! Congratulations, that is, if this even matters to you. One survey found that many vegetarians—even ethical vegetarians—did not care whether or not their choices saved lives! They were ethically opposed to the meat industry and didn't want to be a part of it, even if their diet choices had no actual impact on the lives of animals. (Hamilton, Eating Death)

Now that we've seen the impact vegetarians have on animals, let's turn to our main question: Who are these people anyway?!

2

WHO'S DITCHING MEAT?

THE DEMOGRAPHICS OF DIET CHANGE

VEGETARIANS NUMBER IN THE MILLIONS IN THE UNITED States. Although individual polls vary, in general about 3 percent of Americans say they never eat red meat, poultry, or fish. A third of those vegetarians—or 1 percent of Americans overall—say they also never eat eggs or dairy. If these numbers are accurate, that would mean there are about nine million vegans and vegetarians in the U.S. And that's not even counting the millions of semi-vegetarians who have cut back on the amount of meat they eat (Humane Research Council, Vegetarianism in the U.S.; Priority Ventures Group; Humane Research Council, How Many Vegetarians; How Many Vegetarians, 2003; How Often Do Americans; How Many Vegetarians, 2000; Stahler, How Many Vegetarians; How Many Vegetarians, 2009; Time/CNN Poll; Rothberger, 2012; Newport).

As you can imagine, vegetarians come in all shapes and sizes. From infants to the elderly, from billionaires to welfare recipients, from carpenters to athletes to computer programmers, vegetarians are everywhere. Although they vary as individuals, as a group they differ in distinct ways from omnivores. Certain types of people are more likely to be vegetarian than others; vegetarians differ from meat-eaters in their political and religious beliefs, personalities, mental health, worldviews, and in numerous other ways. Not only are these differences interesting in themselves, they should also matter a lot to anyone who wants to inspire more people to go vegetarian.

WHY IT MATTERS

For-profit companies that want people to buy their products don't advertise at random. They focus on their target audiences, who are the people most likely to respond to their advertising and are most likely to buy their products. Nike, for instance, is not going to advertise basketball sneakers in the magazine published by the American Association of Retired Persons. Most AARP readers aren't in the market for expensive high-tops. Lexus is not going to run advertisements on Nickelodeon, a children's television station, because most Nickelodeon viewers aren't old enough to drive.

In an ideal world for Lexus or Nike, these companies could advertise their products anywhere they wanted and sell just as many cars and sneakers. But neither they, nor we, live in that world. Different types of people have different interests. So for-profit companies focus intently on figuring out their target audience, the people most likely to buy their product. What gender, income-level, ages, and ethnic groups are most likely to buy a Lexus? Do they live in the city, the suburbs, or in rural areas—on the coasts or in the Midwest? Success for a for-profit company involves figuring out the target audience and reaching them.

It isn't only companies that are doing this. In the weeks following the 2012 U.S. presidential election, newspapers reported on a little-known component essential to President Obama's victory: the intense data analysis his campaign used to identify and target swing voters.

Here's what it looked like on the ground. First, a team of fifty analysts spent months compiling information about individual voters in battleground states. They collected everything from age to household income to voting history to what magazines these voters subscribed to. Up to *eighty* separate pieces of information were collected about each voter. Using that information, a mathematical model was created to predict how likely any person was to vote for Obama. The campaign then individually targeted hundreds of thousands of voters who, according to the model, were unsure of whom to cast their ballot for but who could be persuaded to do so for the Democratic candidate. The rest, as they say, is history. Nearly every swing state went to Obama, and he cruised to an easy re-election.

If companies who focus on target audiences make more money, and if politicians who identify specific voters get more votes, advocates of vegetarian eating should be using the same strategy to save more animals. Once they've figured out which groups are most likely to go vegetarian, they can target their advocacy efforts toward them. The result will be a higher rate of success and many more animals spared from a lifetime of misery.

So, who exactly is most likely to go vegetarian?

AGE

Vegetarianism is a young person's game. People under 30 are much more likely to be vegetarian than those who are older. And this isn't a new phenomenon: studies over the past two decades have consistently found the same results.

Among those under 30, is there an ideal age for ditching meat? There may be, but we don't know what it is, yet. Studies on vegetarianism cluster respondents in different ways. Groups found to have the highest rates of vegetarianism have included 18–34 year olds, 18–19 year olds, 20–29 year olds, 18–29 year olds, 18–24 year olds, 15–24 year olds, and 13–15 year olds. Some of these groups were two to three times more likely than any other age group to have gone vegetarian (Humane Research Council, Advocating Meat Reduction; Lea, Moving From Meat; USA: Research Suggest; Humane Research Council, How Many Vegetarians; VegSocUK Information Sheet; How Many Vegetarians, 2000; Haddad and Tanzman, 2003; Americans Pick Ronald McDonald).

When we dig a little deeper into the data, we find that young people might be even more likely to ditch meat—compared to older people—than these numbers suggest. A big problem with studies about vegetarianism is that many researchers and pollsters simply ask people if they're vegetarian. They don't define what the word *vegetarian* means. And as we'll discuss later in this chapter, most people who say they're vegetarian still eat meat. This is particularly true for older people.

A U.S. study revealed that people 50 or older were two to four times more likely to say they were vegetarian when they weren't (Haddad and Tanzman 2003). A Finnish study of nearly 25,000 people found that senior citizens were ten times more likely than 18–29 year olds to say they were vegetarian when they weren't. Adults aged 30–59 were three times more likely than the under-30 crowd to say they were vegetarian when they weren't. (If you categorize pescatarians as vegetarians, then senior citizens were just five times more likely, and 30–59 year olds were just one and a half times more likely, to say they were vegetarian when they weren't.) (Vinnari *et al.* 2008)

As a result of this inaccurate reporting, occasionally a poll comes out that suggests senior citizens or people in their forties are the age groups most likely to be vegetarian (Time/CNN Poll; Humane Research Council, How Many Vegetarians; White *et al.* 1999; Haddad and Tanzman 2003; Newport). This is simply not the case. When we look at all of the studies together, and factor in misreporting, it's clear that young people are more likely to be vegetarian than any other age group.

Now that we've determined that young people are more likely to ditch meat, what does this information suggest for advocates of vegetarianism? One thing it means is that young people should also be more likely to go vegetarian if encouraged to do so. In other words, they are probably a good target audience for vegetarian advocacy. Research still needs to be done to confirm the hypothesis, but the experience of most vegetarian advocacy groups suggests it's true. As a result, most American vegetarian advocacy groups focus their outreach on teenagers and college students.

The fact that young people are an ideal target audience is good news. For one thing, young people are easier to target than other age groups. Colleges, high schools, and many music concerts have a uniformly youthful audience. Because they're more active online, young people are also the easiest age group to reach through social media. Because they're very social and open to new ideas, this age group might be most likely to influence their peers to change their diet.

Finally, young people have their entire meat-eating life ahead of them. Getting someone to go (and stay) vegetarian at 15 years old will spare a lot more animals than getting someone who is aged 50 to do the same. Young vegetarians also have many more years to influence friends and family members to make the switch.

The bottom line? When it comes to promoting vegetarian eating, young people are an ideal audience. Focusing time, money, and energy on getting them to go vegetarian should create many more vegetarians, and spare many more farm animals, than targeting the public as a whole.

GENDER

Women are much, much more likely than men to go vegetarian. There are two to three times as many female vegetarians as there are male vegetarians.

In a representative sampling of studies, women made up the following percentages of vegetarians: 45, 50, 63, 63, 67, 67, 67, 67, 74, 75, 75, 78, 78, and 80 (Ruby 2012; Perry *et al.* 2001; Stahler, How Many Youth; Humane Research Council, Advocating Meat Reduction; Time/CNN Poll; Vegetarian Foods—U.S.; Humane Research Council, Why or Why Not Vegetarian; Humane Research Council, How Many Vegetarians; Ruby and Heine, 2011; Rozin *et al.* 2003; Gale *et al.* 2007; Phillips *et al.* 2011; Santos and Booth 1996; Bas *et al.* 2005).

Female vegetarians outnumber male vegetarians all over the world. The studies mentioned above cover the U.S., Canada, the United Kingdom, the Netherlands, Australia, and other nations. One of the studies surveyed students from eleven different Eurasian countries, and found women accounted for 75 percent of vegetarians (Phillips *et al.* 2011). Even in Swaziland, women remain about twice as likely as men to go veg (Yasmin and Mavuso 2009).

Female vegetarians also outnumber their male counterparts at a roughly even amount in all age groups. Since young people are more likely to not eat meat than older people, young women should be more likely to be vegetarian than any other age and gender group. Indeed, studies have consistently found that to be the case (Beardsworth and Keil 1991; Humane Research Council, Advocating Meat Reduction; Lea, Moving From Meat; USA: Research Suggest; Humane Research Council, How Many Vegetarians; Haddad and Tanzman 2003; Number of UK Vegetarians; Maurer).

Clearly, young women are really the ideal target audience for vegetarian advocates. In Chapter 5 we'll take a closer look at why it's so important to focus on them. We'll also take a look at why there's such a big difference between women and men when it comes to eating meat.

One final note on gender: the gap narrows when it comes to veganism. The number of male and female vegans seems to be fairly equal, both in the United States and in the European Union (Phillips *et al.* 2011; How Many Adults Are Vegan).

INCOME

Are wealthier people more likely to go vegetarian? It's hard to say.

Some studies found that those with middle to higher incomes are more likely to be vegetarian, but other studies discovered no difference (Beardsworth and Bryman 2004; Gale *et al.* 2007; How Often Do Americans; Public Attitudes/ Consumer Behavior). One U.S. poll and one Finnish study even reported that those at the lowest income levels were most likely to say they were vegetarian (Vinnari 2010; Time/CNN Poll). And a recent American poll found that the likelihood of being vegetarian dropped off sharply for those making $100,000 or more, though the small size of that poll means the result could be a statistical error (How Often Do Americans).

At this point, it's impossible to tell whether income is related to vegetarian eating.

EDUCATION

Education does make a difference. People with more education are more likely to go vegetarian.

A very substantial British study, a nationally representative U.S. poll, and several other polls have all found that people who have college degrees are more likely to not eat meat than people without them (Time/CNN Poll; Gale *et al.* 2007; How Often Do Americans; How Many Vegetarians, 2003). A large-scale Finnish study suggested that people with a high level of education were three times more likely to be vegetarian than those with low levels of education. People with moderate levels of education fell in between. The study also found that people with less education were more likely to say they were vegetarian when they still ate meat (Vinnari *et al.* 2008).

If vegetarians are better educated than meat-eaters, shouldn't they also have higher incomes? After all, education and income levels are closely related. Some studies suggest that this could be the case, but career choice might also have an impact. Vegetarians are much more likely to work in the nonprofit, governmental, or education fields, which usually pay less than the private sector (Gale *et al.* 2007; Freeland-Graves *et al.*, A Demographic and Social Profile). So it's possible that vegetarians, while being better educated, still don't make more money than their meat-eating counterparts.

ETHNICITY

It's hard to say which race or ethnic group in America is most likely to be vegetarian. A Time/CNN poll found Caucasians to be slightly more likely than African-Americans, and significantly more likely than Hispanics, to be vegetarian. But a series of national polls commissioned by the Vegetarian Resource Group has found the opposite. Their polls, conducted every few years for the past decade, consistently find Hispanics to be the group most likely to say they don't eat red meat, poultry, or fish. African-Americans usually come in second, with Caucasians typically coming in last. In some of the polls there is a big difference between ethnicities, in others it's a narrow margin. All of the polls have fairly large margins of error (How Often Do Americans; How Many Vegetarians, 2000; How Many Vegetarians, 2003; How Many Vegetarians, 2009; Stahler, How Many Vegetarians).

Other evidence exists that shows that Caucasians may be the most reluctant to give up meat. Three separate studies found that African-Americans were bigger believers in the health benefits and other benefits of vegetarian eating (Meat Consumption Among Whites; Rimal 2002; Kalof *et al.* 1999). Another study suggested that Hispanics were twice as likely as Caucasians to say they used meat alternatives. African-Americans also reported higher than average consumption of a number of vegetarian meat products (Heller). And both African-Americans and Hispanics have a more favorable view of vegetarians than Caucasians (Americans Pick Ronald McDonald).

On the other hand, the higher rates of vegetarianism among Hispanics and African-Americans could be a mirage. As we mentioned earlier, people with lower levels of education are more likely to say they are vegetarian when they are not. In the U.S., African-Americans have lower levels of education than Caucasians. Hispanics have the lowest education levels of all (United States Census Bureau). So the high rates of vegetarianism reported by Hispanics and African-Americans could be inaccurate.

Indeed, one large-scale study of adolescents in the Minneapolis-St. Paul area found that African-American students were more than three times as likely as white students to call themselves vegetarian when they still ate chicken or fish (Perry *et al.* 2001). In that study, about 2.5 percent of white students, 2 percent of Asian students and .5 percent of African-American students were actual vegetarians. Similarly, a 1994 Roper Poll conducted through face-to-face interviews found that although African-Americans were as likely as Caucasians to give up red meat, they were dramatically less likely to give up poultry (Stahler, How Many Vegetarians).

One 2013 U.S. poll, carried out through automated telephone calls, found a jaw-dropping 44 percent of Hispanics saying they were vegetarian or vegan (8 percent of Caucasians and 9 percent of African-Americans made a similar claim). Clearly, many Hispanics either didn't understand what "vegetarian" and "vegan" meant, or they weren't answering honestly (Americans Pick Ronald McDonald). This might explain why other surveys also found Hispanics were most likely to say they were vegetarian.

The bottom line? It's hard to tell how African-Americans, Caucasians, and Hispanics stack up when it comes to vegetarian eating. Not only is it hard to tell who comes out on top, it's also unclear how much of a difference there is between them. Taking in all of the studies we covered, here's a best guess at a conclusion: Caucasians are probably a bit more likely to be vegetarian than African-Americans, and we have no idea how either group compares with Hispanics.

Of course, the real winners of the vegetarian race, as it were, are South and East Asians. Both groups have much higher percentages of vegetarians (How Many Vegetarians, 2000; Time/CNN Poll; Spencer *et al.* 2007) than the other ethnicities. They represent somewhat unique groups, however, since they currently make up only a small minority of the U.S. population (although East Asians had reached nearly 5 percent by 2010), and their vegetarianism is closely linked with religious tradition.

In the U.K., a 2010 survey found that non-Caucasians were much more likely to be vegetarian than Caucasians, with a whopping 12 percent to 4 percent lead. Most of the non-Caucasians who were vegetarian were motivated by religious reasons (Public Attitudes/Consumer Behavior).

GEOGRAPHY

Americans in the Northeast and on the west coast are more likely to be vegetarian than those in the Midwest or South (Stahler, How Often Do Americans; How Many Vegetarians, 2003; How Many Vegetarians, 2009; Stahler, How Many Vegetarians; Americans Pick Ronald McDonald). They are also more likely to prefer meatless meals (Rimal 2002). In the U.K., those living in London and the south of England are most likely to be vegetarian, followed by East Anglia and the Midlands. Residents of northern England and Scotland are least likely to have ditched meat (VegSocUK Information Sheet).

In both the U.S. and other countries, those living in urban areas seem more likely to be vegetarian (Michalak 2012; Hoek *et al.* 2004; Lindeman 2002; How Many Vegetarians, 2000; Baines *et al.* 2007; VegSocUK Information Sheet). They are also more likely to enjoy vegetarian meats (Hoek *et al.* 2004; de Boer and Aiking 2011). One U.S. poll found that 5 percent of people in large cities were vegetarian, compared to 2 percent in the suburbs, 2 percent in rural areas, and a .5 percent in small cities (How Many Vegetarians, 2000). Those living in rural areas are the least likely to believe that being vegetarian helps animals (Kalof *et al.* 1999).

How do rates of vegetarianism compare around the globe? Here's how some nations stack up, from the most to least vegetarian-friendly. Keep in mind that most of these are *self-reported* rates of vegetarianism, which tend to be two to three times higher than actual rates.

COUNTRY	REPORTED (%)	ACTUAL (%)
India		20–42
Italy	10	
Germany	8–9	2
Brazil	8	
United Kingdom	7–11	3
United States	7	2–3
Israel	7	
Australia	5	2
Switzerland	5	
The Netherlands	4.5	
Sweden	4	
Norway	4	
Canada	4	
Austria	3	
Finland	3	0.5–1.5
Turkey	2.5	
France	2	
Belgium	2	
New Zealand	1–2	
Portugal		0.3

(Vegetarians Around the World; Vegetarianism by Country; Priority Ventures Group; Rothberger 2012; How Often Do Americans; How Many Vegetarians 2003; How Many Vegetarians 2009; Michalak 2012; Vinnari 2010; Statistics)

VEGETARIANS: THEY LOVE THEIR MEAT!

Just how many vegetarians are there in the U.S.? Ask a couple of hundred Americans if they're vegetarian, and somewhere between 2 percent and 7 percent will say "yes." Most current studies show that figure to be close to 7 percent (Dietz *et al.* 1995; Humane Research Council, How Many Vegetarians). But is that really true? Are there really almost 20 million vegetarians in the United States?

Unfortunately no, not even close. The majority of people who call themselves vegetarian eat meat—and some of them eat a lot of it! Between 60 percent and 90 percent of so-called vegetarians have consumed flesh in the previous days, week, or month (Humane Research Council, Vegetarianism in the U.S.; White *et al.* 1999; Corliss; Barr and Chapman 2002; Vinnari *et al.* 2008; Haddad and Tanzman 2003; Dietz *et al.* 1995).

Vegetarians aren't the only ones with a curious definition of the words *meat* or *vegetarian*, though. A British study from the 1990s found that only 80 percent of meat-eaters considered chicken or bacon to be meat, only 60 percent considered sausages or burgers to be meat, and only 20 percent considered fish to be meat (Heller).

Chicken and fish are the main meats that self-identified vegetarians are chowing down on. Most studies have found that about two-thirds of those who call themselves vegetarian eat chicken and 80 percent eat fish, although a couple of studies have shown much lower percentages (Dietz *et al.* 1995; Gale *et al.* 2007; Vinnari *et al.* 2008; Michalak *et al.* 2012; Gossard and York 2003; Aston *et al.* 2012; Izmirli and Phillips 2011; White *et al.* 1999; Haddad and Tanzman 2003; Krizmanic). Only one out of every five self-proclaimed vegetarians still eats red meat (Barr and Chapman 2002; Krizmanic).

A thin silver lining with all of these meat-eating vegetarians is that they're eating less meat than the average person. One study discovered that self-defined vegetarians who still ate chicken consumed 30 percent less of it than omnivores (Vinnari *et al.* 2008). A national U.S. health study, carried out in the mid-1990s, found that self-defined vegetarians who still ate meat ingested about 40 percent less red meat and 25 percent less chicken than omnivores. Overall, these wannabe vegetarians ate about 25 percent less meat than omnivores. That percentage would be higher if not for the fact that, in this study, so-called vegetarians consumed nearly twice as much fish as omnivores (Haddad and Tanzman 2003).

A large-scale Finnish study showed similar though less dramatic results: vegetarians who ate meat consumed about 40 percent more fish than omnivores (Vinnari *et al.* 2008; Aston *et al.* 2012). A study of female college students found omnivores, semi-vegetarians, and pescatarians all ate about the same amount of fish (Forestell *et al.* 2012).

Why does fish have such a strong appeal for people who are cutting out other types of meat? For one thing, people have less empathy for fish. They perceive fish as less like us than other animals. They see them as less intelligent and less able to feel pleasure, pain, and other emotions (Harrison 2010; Westbury and Neumann 2008). But pescatarians have a number of other rationales for continuing to eat fish. One study indicated the most common reasons were that pescatarians were concerned about their health if they didn't eat any meat, that eating fish was convenient, that they believed fish wasn't meat, that fishing was better than factory farming, and that consuming fish was a transition to genuine vegetarianism (McPherson).

We've now looked at red meat, chicken, and fish. How do vegetarians—whether real or imagined—match up against omnivores when it comes to eggs and dairy? In the large-scale U.S. health study, self-defined vegetarians who still ate meat consumed the same amount of dairy products as omnivores. Real vegetarians consumed less dairy than average, although that figure may be deceptive since the "vegetarian" group in this study likely included both vegetarians and vegans (Haddad and Tanzman 2003).

The large-scale Finnish study suggested that real vegetarians, meat-eating "vegetarians," and omnivores all consumed the same amount of dairy. It found only a slight difference in egg consumption: real and self-identified vegetarians ate about 5 percent more eggs (Vinnari *et al.* 2008).

One study of U.S. medical school students reported that vegetarians consumed dairy products about 25 percent more often than non-vegetarians (Spencer *et al.* 2007). The study didn't measure total volume, just how often dairy products were consumed. Since these results differ from the results of the large national surveys, any actual difference could be specific to this demographic group.

To close this somewhat depressing section on a positive note, here's a final interesting tidbit about vegetarians. Studies suggest that there are twice as many "vegetarians when dining out" as there are actual vegetarians. Although 3 percent of Americans say they never eat meat, fish, or poultry, national polls conducted in 1999 and 2008 both found that 6–7 percent of Americans say they never eat meat, fish, or poultry when dining out (How Many People). Perhaps these are statistical anomalies; the studies do have margins of error of 3 percentage points. Or perhaps people are misreporting how they eat when dining out. But at face value, the studies suggest there's something about dining out that makes people want to eat a meat-free meal.

SEMI-VEGETARIANS

While they haven't taken the full plunge into a meat-free diet, semi-vegetarians—those who are eating less meat or who have cut out certain kinds of meat—have become major players when it comes to cruelty-free dining.

The number of people who say they are cutting back on meat is about four times larger than the number of people who say they have become vegetarians. Most national surveys have found anywhere from a quarter to a third of the population reporting they are eating less meat now than they used to (Humane Research Council, Advocating Meat Reduction; Research Adds Weight; Rimal 2002; Priority Ventures Group; Heller; Rothberger 2012). While it would be wonderful if that were true, it's not.

Polls from the 1980s to today have consistently found 20–40 percent of the public telling researchers they are cutting back on meat. These include both American and European studies. Yet most of these polls were conducted at a time when average meat consumption was rising year after year (Rothberger 2012; Holm and Mohl 2000; VegSocUK Information Sheet). One U.K. study suggested that less than a quarter of the number of people who said they were cutting back on meat had actually done so. Most of the others had simply been substituting chicken or fish for red meat (Heller).

Over-reporting aside, a lot more people are actually reducing meat intake than those who are actually vegetarian. A 2005 Humane Research Council study suggested that 13 percent of Americans claimed they were eating meat at fewer than half of their meals. By 2011, 16 percent of Americans were stating that fewer than half of their meals contained red meat, chicken, or fish (How Many Adults, 2006). Although these figures probably include over-reporting as well, they should be more accurate than polls that simply ask, "Are you eating less meat?"

If you're curious as to how large an impact semi-vegetarians have far farm animals, you need look no further than the latest meat-consumption trends. As we've seen, per capita meat consumption in the U.S. dropped nearly 10 percent between 2006 and 2012. And it wasn't just red meat consumption that was going down; pork, beef, chicken, and turkey all took a hit. Demand for meat also fell, though not quite as dramatically (Sethu, Meat Consumption). And just who was driving this decline? Semi-vegetarians.

While rates of vegetarianism seem to have increased between 2006 and 2012, that increase is nowhere near large enough to account for a 10 percent drop in meat consumption. The vast majority of that decline has to be due to semi-vegetarians who are scaling back the amount of meat they eat.

Even manufacturers are taking notice. Vegetarian meat producers are now targeting their products toward semi-vegetarians, since they make up a larger share of new customers than vegetarians and vegans (Consumers Prefer Meat-Free).

So just who are these semi-vegetarians? Although we don't have as much data on them as we do on vegetarians, there are a few things we do know.

Semi-vegetarians are similar to vegetarians in a number of ways. For example, women predominate. Women are two to three times more likely than men to be semi-vegetarians (Perry *et al.* 2001; Humane Research Council, Advocating Meat Reduction; Humane Research Council, How Many Vegetarians; Wyker and Davison 2010; Worsley and Skrzypiec 1998). People who are single, people who have no children, and people who have a college education are also all slightly more likely to enjoy meatless meals (Rimal 2002). And two studies found that, like vegetarians, semi-vegetarians are more likely to care about their health and to embrace values of equality and compassion for all (Lea, Moving From Meat; de Boer *et al.* 2007).

Vegetarians and semi-vegetarians may differ when it comes to age, though. Young people are more likely than any other age group to be vegetarian, but they are less likely to say they're cutting back on meat than other age groups. (Still, even among young people there are more semi-vegetarians than full vegetarians.) (Perry *et al.* 2001; Haddad and Tanzman 2003) So which age group is the cream of the crop when it comes to semi-vegetarianism? Older individuals, particularly those 55 years of age and above, are most likely to say they've cut back on meat (Stahler, How Often Do Americans; Humane Research Council, Advocating Meat Reduction). But this may well be just another case of older people over-reporting dietary change. As a result, we really can't tell which age group is most likely to cut back on meat. It does seem, though, that young people don't enjoy the commanding lead they do when it comes to full vegetarianism.

It's also unclear if income level is related to going semi-vegetarian. Two studies found that semi-vegetarians are more likely to have lower income levels or, if teenagers, to come from families with lower income levels (Stahler, How Often Do Americans; Perry *et al.* 2001). On the other hand, a recent Finnish study discovered that those most likely to replace red meat with chicken (a type of semi-vegetarianism that actually hurts animals) were mainly from the middle class. And another study suggested that people with high incomes were more likely to be semi-vegetarian. In this study, as income levels increased, so did the chances that a person was eating more meatless meals than before (Rimal 2002).

3

WHAT SETS THEM APART

HOW TO PICK A VEGETARIAN OUT OF A CROWD

VEGETARIANS ARE DEMOCRATS

Democrats are more likely than Republicans to be vegetarian. Although some polls show little difference in political and dietary affiliation, others suggest Democrats are twice as likely to have ditched meat (Time/CNN Poll; Spencer *et al.* 2007; White *et al.* 1999, Rao *et al.* 2010; Americans Pick Ronald McDonald). They are also much more likely than Republicans or Independents to have a favorable view of vegetarians (Americans Pick Ronald McDonald).

We should note that when it comes to political beliefs—and everything else in this chapter—we're not arguing that the two are causally related. In other words, we're not saying that being a vegetarian makes you become a Democrat, or that being a Democrat turns you into a vegetarian. It's possible that one of those could be true. It's also possible that both are caused by something else entirely, such as whether you live in an urban area or not.

All we're saying is that the two traits are correlated. As a result, advocates of vegetarian eating will probably inspire more people to go vegetarian if they focus on Democrats than if they target the public as a whole. The same applies for focusing on any of the other demographic groups listed below. These types of people are more likely to be vegetarian. Therefore, we are assuming that members of these groups are also more likely to go vegetarian if encouraged to do so.

VEGETARIANS AREN'T MARRIED

Single people are much more likely to be vegetarian than married people. Studies suggest they're more than twice as likely to be meat-free (Vinnari *et al.* 2008; Newport).

Single people are also more likely to enjoy meat-free meals (Rimal 2002). Divorced, widowed, and co-habiting people are also significantly more likely than married people to be vegetarian (Vinnari *et al.* 2008).

VEGETARIANS ARE MIDDLE CHILDREN

One study revealed that vegetarians were more likely to be middle children than meat-eaters. They were less likely to be first-born or only children (Freeland-Graves *et al.*, A Demographic and Social Profile).

VEGETARIANS ARE LGBT

There are not a lot of data on the subject, but LGBT Americans may be more likely to go vegetarian than their straight counterparts. A study of women forty and older compared the eating habits of lesbians with the eating habits of their straight, similar-age sisters. While 8.5 percent of straight women said they were vegetarian at some point in the previous year, among lesbians that number rose to 10.7 percent (Roberts *et al.* 2003).

VEGETARIANS GREW UP WITH MORE COMPANION ANIMALS

A survey of British college students in the 1990s found that those who had grown up with two or more important companion animals were almost twice as likely to avoid eating some or all animal products for ethical reasons. (In this study, "important" companion animals were animals the person felt they had a meaningful relationship with.)

The link was particularly strong for women; there was only a slight connection among men. Women who grew up with many companion animals, whether important or not, were also more likely to avoid eating some or all animal products.

The study's authors weren't able to tell whether having companion animals caused people to go vegetarian, or if both the vegetarianism and the living with companion animals were influenced by something else (Paul and Serpell 1993).

VEGETARIANS ARE SMART

A bold statement, sure, but the research backs it up. One study indicated that kids who had a higher IQ at age ten were more likely to be vegetarians by the time they reached mid-adulthood. This was true regardless of how much education they received, their social class, and their gender. The trend also held true for both actual vegetarians and for people who called themselves vegetarian but still ate meat.

A large-scale study of adults found that vegetarians had, on average, a five-point higher IQ score than meat-eaters (Richards 2007; Gale *et al.* 2007).

VEGETARIANS ARE INTROVERTED

If you were trying to guess the Myers-Briggs personality type of a vegetarian, starting off with an "I" for introverted would be a good bet. Several studies have found vegetarians to be slightly more introverted than meat-eaters (Forestell *et al.* 2012; Cooper *et al.* 1985).

Interestingly, that introversion seems to be related to how and when that individual goes vegetarian. A 2012 study suggested that vegetarians who made the switch for ethical reasons were more likely to be introverted than those who made the switch for health-related reasons. It also found that vegetarians who were introverts ditched meat earlier in their lives than vegetarians who weren't introverted (Bobic *et al.* 2012).

Remember, this doesn't mean that introversion causes people to go vegetarian. It might. But it's also possible that something else causes people to both be introverted and go vegetarian. All we're saying is that introverts are a bit more likely to be vegetarian than extroverts.

VEGETARIANS ARE ARTISTIC

An old study of vegetarians from the 1980s found that they were more likely to describe themselves as having artistic traits (Freeland-Graves *et al.*, A Demographic and Social Profile). A more recent study found that the personality trait of imaginativeness was related to a greater concern for animal welfare (Mathews and Herzog 1997).

Maybe that same artistic nature that causes vegetarians to be more Mac-inclined than their meat-eating counterparts. (Macs have a reputation, whether deserved or undeserved, of being the ideal computer for the artistically inclined.) According to a Hunch.com survey of hundreds of thousands of readers, Mac users are 80 percent more likely than PC users to be vegetarian (Mac vs. PC). Of course, maybe vegetarians are just buying Macs because they want to pay tribute to one of their own: Apple founder Steve Jobs was meat-free for most of his adult life.

VEGETARIANS ARE AS FRIENDLY AND ACTIVE AS MEAT-EATERS

A study of Scandinavian teenagers found that those who ate little to no meat and those who were omnivores belonged to the same number of clubs and organizations, spent the same number of nights out with friends, and had the same number of close friends. They also exercised about the same amount and were equally involved in virtually every sport measured: walking, cycling, dancing, running, gymnastics, weight lifting, soccer, ice hockey, basketball, tennis, horseback riding, track and field, martial arts, and skiing (Larsson *et al.* 2002).

An older American study discovered that vegetarians were more likely than meat-eaters to join every type of organization the study measured, including self-help groups and civic, social, and religious organizations. Vegetarians were also more likely than meat-eaters to go out with friends and to have guests over (Freeland-Graves *et al.*, A Demographic and Social Profile). So while they may be a bit introverted, vegetarians clearly aren't shut-ins.

VEGETARIANS DON'T FOLLOW TRADITIONAL RELIGIONS

Compared to meat-eaters, vegetarians are much less likely to follow traditional Western religions like Protestantism, Catholicism, Islam, and Judaism. Vegetarians are less likely to belong to a congregation, and are more likely to have never attended religious services (Freeland-Graves *et al.*, A Demographic and Social Profile).

One study suggested that the more regularly a person attends church, the less likely they are to extend moral concern to animals (Kruse 1999). One reason for this discrepancy may be because, although religious people see animals as intelligent and valuable, they don't see them as being on an evolutionary continuum with humans. Instead, they see animals as being fundamentally different (Templer *et al.* 2006).

Vegetarians are much more likely than meat-eaters to be atheists or agnostics. They're also more likely to follow non-monotheistic religions such as Buddhism (Freeland-Graves *et al.*, A Demographic and Social Profile). One British study suggested that vegetarians were several times more likely than omnivores to join new religious sects or cults (Hamilton 2000).

VEGETARIAN ADULTS DRINK AND SMOKE LESS

Vegetarian adults are much less likely than meat-eaters to smoke cigarettes or drink alcohol (Aston *et al.* 2012; Freeland-Graves *et al.*, A Demographic and Social Profile; Spencer *et al.* 2007; Haddad and Tanzman 2003). The substance-free policy doesn't always hold true though: at least as of the 1980s, vegetarians used drugs slightly more often than non-vegetarians (Freeland-Graves *et al.*, Health Practices). A 2003 study showed that, although they still consumed less alcohol overall, vegetarians drank more than twice as much wine as meat-eaters (Haddad and Tanzman 2003).

VEGETARIANS AREN'T FOODIES

Okay, it's true that vegetarians can be a bit food-obsessed. There's little they love more than sharing photos of their latest meal or talking about how great some new vegetarian restaurant is. But according to one study, vegetarians and foodies are quite distinct groups. The study suggested that foodies tend to be people who are making more money than their parents, who have moved into major urban areas, and who intently seek out experiences that stimulate the senses. Vegetarians on the other hand are not upwardly mobile, they tend already to come from cities, and they're not as concerned with new taste experiences. Foodies are also more likely than vegetarians to surround themselves with friends who have a similar diet and social background to them (Back and Glasgow 1981).

PEOPLE WILLING TO PURCHASE "HUMANE" MEAT ARE MORE LIKELY TO GO VEGETARIAN

A national U.S. poll carried out by the Humane Research Council found there was an overlap between vegetarians, semi-vegetarians, and people willing to spend more for "humane" animal products. Consumers who were willing to pay more for "humane" products were more likely than the general public to be willing to go vegetarian or semi-vegetarian. They were also more likely than the general public to already be vegetarian or semi-vegetarian (Humane Research Council, Advocating Meat Reduction). Similarly, a Dutch study indicated that people who bought free-range meat tended to eat less meat overall (de Boer *et al.* 2007).

Some animal advocates cast particularly dirty looks at people who have switched to organic, free-range, or cage-free animal products. These studies should come as encouraging news to them. "Humane" eaters are more likely than the general public to be willing to go vegetarian or cut back on meat consumption if shown why and how to do so.

4

THIS IS YOUR BRAIN ON TOFU

THE HEARTS AND MINDS OF VEGETARIANS

THE CARING VEGETARIAN

"There are more important problems to worry about than animals."

If you're a vegetarian, you've probably heard these words more times than you care to count. Some meat-eaters seem to think that not only is it silly to care about animals, but that if you do it means that you're less concerned than they are about human suffering.

The idea isn't new. A prominent psychiatrist of the 1940s argued that vegetarians were sadistic and cared little about the suffering of other people (Barahal 1946). While not quite as derogatory, a 2010 British study discovered the public still thought animal advocates had below-average empathy toward human beings (Knight *et al.* 2010).

Recent studies, however, suggest that vegetarians are more empathetic than meat-eaters toward both humans *and* animals. In one study, vegetarians and omnivores were placed in a fMRI machine. These machines, like typical MRIs, use magnetic imaging essentially to photograph the inside of a body. What makes fMRIs unique is they focus on the flow of blood. Because extra blood flows to the parts of the brain we're using at any given time, fMRIs are a good way to measure brain activity. They can show what regions of the brain are being activated, and how strongly.

In this study, vegetarians, vegans, and omnivores were placed in an fMRI machine and shown a series of pictures. Some of the pictures were of natural landscapes, but the majority were scenes involving human or animal suffering: pictures of mutilations, dead bodies, wounds, and threats to humans and animals. The fMRI machines scanned the subjects' brains to see how the blood flowed through them after viewing each picture. The goal of the study was to see what reaction the pictures would generate among people with different diets.

Researchers found that the areas of the brain associated with empathy lit up more widely and more intensely in vegetarians and vegans. This was true not just for the pictures of animal suffering, but for the pictures of human misery as well. Those who did not eat meat seemed to react more strongly to human and animal suffering than meat-eaters. Interestingly, vegetarians and vegans responded somewhat differently from one another, although they both had a stronger response than omnivores.

The study also gave participants a written survey designed to measure their empathy for others. The results matched the brain scans. Vegetarians and vegans scored higher on the empathy scale than people who ate meat (Filippi *et al.* 2010).

A separate study revealed similar results: vegetarians had more empathy than meat-eaters toward both companion animals and people (Preylo and Arkiwawa 2008). Interestingly, this study suggested that while female vegetarians were only slightly more caring than female omnivores, there was a dramatic difference among men. Compared to their meat-eating counterparts, vegetarian men were much more likely to put themselves in another's shoes, and to feel empathy and distress for others.

Another study showed that vegetarians were much more altruistic than meat-eaters. In fact, for every point up the altruism scale a respondent went, their likelihood of being a vegetarian quadrupled (Kalof *et al.* 1999). This altruism might explain why, in another study, vegetarians were four times as likely as meat-eaters to be working for a nonprofit organization (Freeland-Graves *et al.*, A Demographic and Social Profile).

Not only do vegetarians have more empathy for animals, they also instinctively respond to them in more social ways. In another fMRI study, participants were shown videos of pigs and monkeys making movements with their mouths. Compared to meat-eaters, vegetarians and vegans had more brain-response activity. This included greater language-network activity in response to the monkey videos, and greater empathy-related responses to the pig videos.

Vegetarians and vegans also had more firing in the parts of the brain associated with mirroring. Mirroring is a crucial part of interpersonal communication. It involves responding to and matching facial, emotional, and interactional cues the other person is giving off. In other words, vegetarians and vegans responded to animals as individuals. They saw pigs and monkeys as more of an "other" and less of an object, than did meat-eaters (Massimo *et al.* 2012).

So feel good about yourselves, vegetarians. As a group, you have more empathy toward both humans and animals. As a group, you are more much more altruistic than average. And as a group, you're more likely to respond to animals as the intelligent, social beings they are.

Of course, you don't want to rub this in the face of meat-eaters!

VEGETARIANS HAVE DIFFERENT VALUES

What sort of people would you expect to be vegetarian? Probably people who say they care more about animal cruelty, health, or the environment, right? It turns out though that people who care more about these things are only slightly more likely to have stopped eating meat (Ogden *et al.* 2007, Kalof *et al.* 1999; Hamilton 2000). Why this discrepancy?

Maybe it's because people's beliefs often don't line up with their behaviors. Consider for example a 2008 poll in which 25 percent of Americans said they believed animals should have the exact same rights as humans to be free from harm and exploitation (Newport, Post-Derby Tragedy). Or consider that 12 percent of Britons say that the slaughter of animals should be banned (VegSocUK Information Sheet). Obviously the vast majority of people who agreed with those statements were meat-eaters. Their stated beliefs and their actions were two different things. So concern about animal cruelty and a desire to eat healthfully aren't necessarily signs that a person is a lot more likely to be vegetarian. But some other values are.

Vegetarians are much less likely than meat-eaters to prioritize what researchers call traditional values: family security, self-discipline, obedience, cleanliness, politeness, honesty, social order, and loyalty. That doesn't mean vegetarians don't care about these things, just that meat-eaters say they care more about them (Dietz *et al.* 1995; Kalof *et al.* 1999; Beardsworth and Bryman 1999).

Similarly, people who embrace authoritarianism are less likely to be vegetarian. Those who support hierarchical social systems, and who want their own group to dominate, are bigger meat-eaters (Chin *et al.* 2002; Ruby and Heine 2011; Allen *et al.* 2000). Vegetarians are more likely to value peace, inner harmony, equality, gender equality, and social justice (Lea, Moving From Meat; de Boer *et al.*, Climate Change and Meat Eating; Allen *et al.* 2000; Worsley and Skrzypiec 2007). Maybe that's why vegetarians are more altruistic and empathetic than meat-eaters.

In one interesting study, participants were told about the connection between authoritarianism and meat-eating. The result? Participants who had said earlier in the study that they were against authoritarianism had a decreased interest in eating meat. In other words when meat was connected with something they opposed, they became less comfortable with eating it (Allen and Baines 2002).

A British study suggested that vegetarians are much more opposed to nuclear weapons and capital punishment, and much more supportive of abortion, than non-vegetarians (Hamilton 2000). They are also more likely to consider other ethical issues when shopping, such as the use of recycled packaging, sustainable production, fair trade, carbon emissions, local versus non-local origin, and whether the product is organic or not (Public Attitudes/Consumer Behavior).

VEGETARIANS AND MENTAL HEALTH

When it comes to mental health and happiness, how do vegetarians stack up against meat-eaters? Unfortunately, not so well. Vegetarians tend to have higher rates of depression, anxiety, and similar mental health issues. Semi-vegetarians have the highest rates of all.

Only two studies found vegetarians to be happier than meat-eaters. One was a study of members of the Seventh Day Adventist Church, a Christian congregation that encourages vegetarian eating. Vegetarian Adventists had less anxiety and depression than meat-eating Adventists. Obviously, these results could be unique to members of this small Christian sect. And because vegetarianism is actively encouraged, Adventist vegetarians are going with the social norm as opposed to against it. So while the results are interesting, they can't be applied to the public as a whole (Michalak *et al.* 2012).

The only other study that found vegetarians to be more mentally healthy was a recent Croatian study. It found vegetarians scored lower on scales of neuroticism and psychosis compared to the general public (Bobic *et al.* 2012).

Nearly every other study on the topic has found vegetarians and semi-vegetarians reporting higher rates of mental disorders. A study of college-age women in the U.S. discovered vegetarians to be slightly more neurotic than omnivores (Forestell *et al.* 2012). A study of teenage vegetarians revealed they were more likely to be hypochondriacs (Cooper *et al.* 1985). A large-scale study of over four thousand American adolescents found that vegetarians were more likely to be depressed, more likely to have thought about killing themselves, and more than twice as likely to have actually tried to commit suicide. Semi-vegetarians were even unhealthier on most of these measures (Perry *et al.* 2001).

In a recent study of vegetarian college students and adults (the average age in the study was twenty-four), vegetarians reported more depression, anxiety, and stress than meat-eaters (Timko *et al.* 2012). A study of Swedish and Norwegian teenagers found that those who ate little or no meat were more likely to be depressed (Larsson *et al.* 2002). And a study from the early 1990s reported that teenagers who had less emotional stability were more likely to avoid at least some meat (Worsley and Skrzypiec 1998).

A Finnish study of high school students concluded that vegetarians had higher rates of distrust, perfectionism, and fears of facing the demands of adult life (Lindeman *et al.* 2000). Another Finnish study, which looked mainly at students, found that vegetarians had lower self-esteem and more depression than meat-eaters. Vegetarians saw the world as less controllable and benevolent, and they viewed people as less benevolent and less just (Lindeman 2002).

As you may have noticed, every one of these studies was focused on young people. Clearly, vegetarians under the age of thirty are more mentally troubled than their meat-eating counterparts. But what about adults? Are vegetarians in their forties and fifties also more likely to have mental health issues?

Probably. A large-scale national health study, which looked at a representative sample of the German population, found vegetarians had higher rates of mental health issues and that vegetarians and semi-vegetarians (as a combined group) had nearly twice the rates of depression, anxiety disorders, and somatoform disorders as meat-eaters. This rate held true even after controlling for other variables, such as age and gender (Michalak *et al.* 2012).

Here's another intriguing question: What comes first? Do the mental health issues precede and possibly inspire people to go vegetarian? Does going vegetarian happen and possibly cause people to have mental health issues? Either seems plausible. People who are depressed or anxious might become more sensitive to the suffering of others, including farm animals. They might also be motivated to change themselves and their diet in a healthier direction. On the other hand, finding out about the terrible cruelties done to farm animals could lead people to go vegetarian and also to become depressed. The sense of isolation from being vegetarian in a decidedly non-vegetarian world could also lead people to become depressed. So, which actually comes first: the depression or the vegetarianism?

The national German study suggested that mental disorders tended to have a much earlier onset than the switch to vegetarianism. The average age at which people went vegetarian or semi-vegetarian was thirty. The average age at which depression or anxiety began was eighteen to twenty-four. So it's possible that mental health issues do indeed push some people toward vegetarian eating. But it's also possible that some personality trait, or some psychological or chemical mechanism, both predisposes people to mental health problems and makes them more likely to go vegetarian.

For example, one study discovered vegetarians are more likely than omnivores to value their emotional states (Allen *et al.* 2000). Sensitive people have been shown to care more about animal welfare, and sensitive people might also be more likely to become anxious or depressed (Mathews and Herzog 1997). So this trait could lead a person toward both vegetarianism and anxiety or depression.

Does going vegetarian have any impact on a person's mental health? If you ask vegetarians, they'll tell you it does. Many vegetarians say their well-being and happiness increased after making the switch (Lindeman 2002). There are certainly emotional reasons why that could be the case. One study suggests the biochemistry of what we eat might play a role as well. In that study, omnivores were split into three groups. One group ate a standard diet for two weeks, one had no meat or poultry but lots of fish, and the third ate only vegetarian fare. After two weeks, the vegetarian group had the largest positive increases in mood. They reported less stress, less tension and anxiety, and more energy than either of the other groups (Beezhold and Johnston 2012).

VEGETARIAN TEENAGERS: REBELS WITH A CAUSE

Depression, anxiety, and neuroticism aren't the only problems young vegetarians face. Whereas vegetarians as a whole drink less alcohol than meat-eaters, one survey of Canadian vegetarian and semi-vegetarian teenagers found they drank alcohol and smoked at nearly twice the rate of non-vegetarians (Greene-Finestone *et al.* 2008). A study of vegetarian female college students revealed they were also more likely to drink and much more likely to smoke, with semi-vegetarians drinking and smoking the most of all (Forestell *et al.* 2012).

Smoking and drinking aren't the only rebellious activities teenage vegetarians get up to. Vegetarian teenagers have also been found to exhibit more at-risk and authority-defying behavior. One study even found they performed more poorly in school, which is interesting given their higher IQs. Vegetarian teenagers are also more likely to have body piercings and tattoos and to believe themselves to be in poor health (Greene-Finestone *et al.* 2008).

When it comes to health-related behaviors like smoking, drinking, and eating poorly, it looks like young vegetarians and old vegetarians have some fundamental differences.

ARE VEGETARIANS DIETERS?

While vegetarianism is often called a "vegetarian diet," are vegetarians more likely than meat-eaters to intentionally cut back on calories?

The data are mixed, and nearly all of the information is confined to teenagers and college students. Several studies on restrained eating have found that young vegetarians actually do it less than meat-eaters. (Restrained eating is the clinical term for dieting; it means regulating how many calories you eat in order to control your weight.) Even people who went vegetarian in part because they wanted to control their weight had less restrained eating than meat-eaters (Perry *et al.* 2001; Forestell *et al.* 2012; Curtis and Comer 2006; Barr *et al.* 1994).

But other studies have come to the opposite conclusion. A pair of studies from Finland found teenage and college-aged vegetarians had higher levels of restrained eating (Lindeman 2002; Lindeman *et al.* 2000). A 2008 study of female ninth graders in Canada discovered that vegetarians were four times as likely to diet to lose weight (Greene-Finestone *et al.*, 2008).

The bottom line is we just don't know whether young vegetarians are more, less, or equally likely to restrict how much food they eat. We also don't know how adult vegetarians stack up against adult omnivores.

One thing we do know, though, is that semi-vegetarians are much more likely to be restrained eaters than the general public. They are more likely to be trying to lose weight, and more likely to use unhealthy weight-control practices (Perry *et al.* 2001; Forestell *et al.* 2012; Lindeman 2002; Lindeman *et al.* 2000; Curtis and Comer 2006; Worsley and Skrzypiec 1997; Greene-Finestone *et al.* 2008; Larsson *et al.*

2002; Mooney and Walbourn 2001; Gilbody *et al.* 1999; Martins *et al.* 1999; Barr *et al.* 1994).

VEGETARIANS MAKE BETTER SEX PARTNERS— MAYBE

There isn't any actual research that directly shows vegetarians make better sex partners. But some evidence suggests they might. In one study, 62 percent of vegetarians said their sex lives improved after they stopped eating meat. Some said they now had more energy and endurance, while others attributed improved sex lives to the emotional benefits of being meat-free (Partridge and Amato).

Vegetarians and meat-eaters seem equally likely to have active sex lives: 40–45 percent of both groups have sex at least once a week (Wolfers). But vegetarians might be less inhibited and more giving in the bedroom. An OKCupid.com analysis of over 250,000 online-dating profiles found that vegetarian women are about twice as likely as meat-eating women to enjoy giving oral sex. Vegetarian men are also more likely to enjoy giving oral sex than their carnivorous competition (Rudder). Maybe that's because, as we saw earlier, vegetarians are more altruistic and empathetic.

But does being more giving really make you a better lover? You bet it does. As one recent study showed, couples who are more focused on one another's pleasure, and who are more giving in bed, are more likely to have a long-lasting, happy, and active sex life (Muise *et al.*).

Moving on, another study suggested that women think vegetarian men smell better than meat-eaters. In this study, men were divided into two groups. One group abstained from meat for two weeks, and the other was fed a more standard diet that included meat. Both groups had to avoid deodorant, smoking, drinking, and eating noxious foods. After the two weeks were up, each man had his armpits swabbed with cotton pads. The pads were then placed in plastic bags, and women smelled the bags and rated the odor of each. The men who had eaten vegetarian for two weeks were rated as having odors that were more attractive, more pleasant, and less intense (Havlicek and Lenochova 2006). So to the extent that attractive body odor makes intimacy more enjoyable, vegetarians have the edge yet again.

While it's outside the scope of this book, one could also point to physiological issues that might make vegetarians better in bed. These include the connection between a fatty, meat-heavy diet and erectile dysfunction, the impact a nutrient-rich vegetarian diet can have on energy and stamina levels, and the fact that vegetarians are less likely to be overweight (Ornish).

Unfortunately for them, meat-eaters are missing out on the action! A recent Match.com survey of four thousand online daters found that a whopping 30 percent of meat-eaters would refuse to date a vegetarian. Only 4 percent of vegetarians said they'd be unwilling to go out with an omnivore (Would You Date a Vegetarian).

STRICT VEGETARIANS HAVE LOTS OF VEGETARIAN FRIENDS AND FAMILY

It's said that you can measure a person by the company they keep. That saying certainly rings true when it comes to vegetarians. Strict vegetarians don't just have a few meat-free friends, they surround themselves with fellow vegetarians.

The only study on vegetarian friendship-patterns dates back to the 1980s, so things may have changed since then. But as of that time, 70 percent of vegans and lacto-vegetarians (vegetarians who avoid eggs but consume dairy) said that at least half their friends were vegetarian. The numbers dropped a bit among those who were less consistent with their diet. Just over a third of pescatarians and vegetarians said at least half their friends were vegetarian. Vegans were the most insular group of all: 40 percent of vegans said that all of their friends were vegan, too (Freeland-Graves *et al.*, A Demographic and Social Profile).

Unfortunately, not every meatless eater is blessed with vegetarian friends. Studies have found that between 4 percent and 8 percent don't have any at all. Pescatarians and vegetarians are the groups most likely to have no vegetarian friends or family members (Lea, Moving From Meat; Freeland-Graves *et al.*, A Demographic and Social Profile).

Having vegetarian friends seems particularly important for men. A 2000 study suggested that the biggest predictor of vegetarianism in men was not how health-conscious they were, how much they were against animal cruelty, or how much they liked or disliked meat. The biggest predictor in men was the number of vegetarian friends they had. So maybe vegetarian men are more likely than vegetarian women to seek out meat-free friends. Or maybe men are particularly likely to stop eating meat if they have friends who've already done so (Lea and Worsley 2001). It's possible vegetarian men feel more comfortable around other vegetarian men because they know their masculinity won't be questioned by them.

It's also interesting to see the friendship difference between current vegetarians and people who say they'd consider going vegetarian. A 2001 study indicated that, while only 4 percent of current vegetarians had no vegetarian friends, over 40 percent of those considering going vegetarian had no vegetarian friends. And almost none of those prospective vegetarians had more than a few vegetarian friends (Lea, Moving From Meat). If they did, maybe they would already be vegetarian!

Knowing a vegetarian does seem particularly helpful for making the switch. In a 1992 study, nearly two-thirds of vegetarians said that knowing another vegetarian was part of what influenced them to make the switch. Similarly, 40 percent of vegetarians said they themselves had inspired a friend or family member to go vegetarian (Powell 2002; Powell, Lifestyle As a Dimension).

So take note, vegetarian advocates: it certainly wouldn't hurt to have as many meat-eating friends as possible! Knowing you might be what helps them over the hump into vegetarianism. And if you're a meat-eater who wants to make the switch, some vegetarian friends could be just what you need.

Just as strict vegetarians have more vegetarian friends, they're also more likely to have vegetarian spouses. One study revealed that 46 percent of vegans were married to a vegan, vegetarian, or pescatarian. Only 12 percent of pescatarians had a meat-free partner (Freeland-Graves *et al.*, A Demographic And Social Profile).

Does vegetarian eating spread through families? It does! One study of Australian teenagers found that only 3 percent of vegetarians and semi-vegetarians had meat-free parents (Worsley and Skrzypiec 1997). But another study discovered that 11 percent of vegetarians said they had parents who were also vegetarian, and 20 percent had vegetarian siblings (Freeland-Graves *et al.*, A Demographic And Social Profile). So just as having a vegetarian friend should make a person more likely to stop eating meat, having vegetarian family members probably has the same effect.

Vegan parents certainly hope that's the case. In one study, 100 percent of vegan parents said they expected their children to stay vegetarian for the rest of their life. Only half of pescatarian parents expected the same (Freeland-Graves *et al.*, A Demographic And Social Profile).

VEGETARIANS ARE PICKY ABOUT
"NON-VEGETARIAN" FOOD

One national U.S. poll found that vegetarians are very picky about eating food that has come into contact with animal products. The poll surveyed two thousand adults and asked those who were vegetarian if they would eat certain foods.

Only about half of them said they'd eat a veggie burger prepared on a grill that meat had been cooked on, even if the grill had been cleaned first. Only one of every five vegetarians (and virtually no vegans) said they'd continue to buy their favorite dessert if they found out the sugar in it had been processed through a filter containing animal bones. And only 4 percent of vegetarians said they'd eat meat grown in a laboratory, even if the animal DNA used to produce the meat had been obtained a full decade ago (Stahler, Sugar).

Unfortunately, the stereotype of vegetarians being difficult guests at barbecues appears to be backed up by the research!

VEGETARIANS AREN'T PERFECT
ON ANIMAL ISSUES

Despite how finicky they are with their food, most vegetarian shoppers aren't fully animal-friendly (even aside from the eggs and dairy). A 1992 study of nearly 600 actual vegetarians found that only half of them avoided leather, and only a third said that the wearing of fur was undesirable. Only about a quarter of respondents refused to buy bath and body products tested on animals (Powell 2002).

Why would this be the case? Probably because many vegetarians stopped eating meat to improve their health. Others did so because they disliked the taste of meat or to protect the environment. These vegetarians simply aren't concerned with reducing their personal impact on animals to the fullest extent possible.

The bottom line is that many vegetarians aren't perfect, and they don't expect others to be either. Nonetheless, they're still doing a tremendous amount of good for animals by leaving meat off their plate.

HOW PEOPLE PERCEIVE VEGETARIANS

What does the general public think about vegetarians? In the West, vegetarians seem to have been digging themselves out of a pretty deep hole over the past few hundred years.

During the Inquisition, vegetarians were seen as heretics. In the 1800s, they were mocked as pale, unhealthy food faddists (Ruby 2012; Maurer). As we saw, in 1946 the head of psychiatry at a major U.S. hospital published a scholarly paper about how vegetarians were domineering and sadistic. They "display little regard for the suffering of their fellow human being," he noted (Barahal 1946).

Things had gotten a lot better by the 1980s. Even then, a U.S. study showed that the public tended to stereotype vegetarians as pacifists, hypochondriacs, drug-users, and weight-conscious liberals. Perhaps these stereotypes weren't too far off the mark. The same study suggested vegetarians viewed themselves as non-competitive, weight-conscious, and having a penchant for drugs. They also viewed themselves as sexy and intellectual (Ruby 2012).

The public has a more positive view of vegetarians now. A 2013 poll found that half of Americans have a favorable opinion about meatless eaters, with only one in five offering an unfavorable view. Hispanics, African-Americans, and Democrats are most likely to think well of vegetarians—two-thirds give them the thumbs up. Young people, women, and those on the west coast are also more likely to think positively about them.

When it comes to people's thoughts on vegans, the same trends hold true. But every demographic group likes vegans less than they like vegetarians. Only 40 percent of Americans have a favorable view of vegans, with 30 percent having an unfavorable view (Americans Pick Ronald McDonald).

Another recent study found the public thinks of vegetarians as generally good but over-sensitive (Ruby and Heine 2011; Minson and Monin 2012). The perception of mental weakness is probably due to the fact that meat is equated with masculinity. A 2011 study showed that both omnivores and vegetarians saw vegetarian men as less masculine (Ruby 2012; Ruby and Heine 2011).

The good news is that both vegetarians and omnivores now see vegetarians as more ethical people than meat-eaters. The perceived difference grows even larger when specific foods like lamb, beef, and chicken are mentioned (Minson and Monin

2012; Ruby and Heine 2011). This change in opinion speaks volumes to how much the culture has shifted: vegetarianism has gone from heresy to stupidity to an admirable moral behavior.

While the general public believes vegetarians are more ethical, vegetarians see a slightly bigger gap between their level of ethics and those of meat-eaters (Bobic *et al.* 2012). It's understandable that vegetarians would feel that way. But if they want to help farm animals, they shouldn't show it. When meat-eaters feel that vegetarians are judging them they become more pro-meat and more anti-vegetarian.

One study found that meat-eaters who think that vegetarians view themselves as the same as or only slightly better than omnivores had the most positive things to say about vegetarians. In other words, they don't think that vegetarians judge them, so they have no need to judge vegetarians back.

But meat-eaters who think vegetarians view themselves as much more ethical than everyone else are defensive. They have a lot more negative things to say about vegetarians. And in one study, when meat-eaters in general were asked to think about vegetarians' moral judgments of them, it caused them to be more derogatory toward vegetarians and more pro-meat. The study also found though that once meat-eaters got the chance to speak badly about vegetarians, their support for meat dropped back to its regular level (Minson and Monin 2012). After they've attacked the messenger, they are more open to the message itself.

This study highlights how counterproductive it is to guilt-trip meat-eaters—a strategy confirmed by other research literature. Guilt-based messages make people even less likely to do what you want them to do (Cooney 2011). The more judged they feel, the more tightly meat-eaters will cling to pro-meat and anti-vegetarian beliefs.

Thankfully, it looks like most vegetarians aren't very judgmental. One study discovered vegetarians look down on meat-eaters three times less than meat-eaters think they do (Minson and Monin 2012). A large study from the 1990s also found vegetarians to be surprisingly non-judgmental. Vegetarians said they were a lot less bothered by people eating meat than they were by people smoking a cigarette or "doing something to harm the environment" (Krizmanic).

5

OH BROTHER

WHY WOMEN ARE MUCH, MUCH MORE
VEG-FRIENDLY THAN MEN

WHEN IT COMES TO VEGETARIAN EATING AND ATTITUDES toward animals, women are much more progressive than men.

It's not just that they are more likely to be vegetarian and semi-vegetarian, although they are. It's not just that they eat a lot less meat, although they do. And it's not just that they care more about animals overall, although they do care more. Counting all of the ways that women are better than men on vegetarian-related issues is like picking the petals off a rose—and there are *a lot* of petals.

Here's the rundown of how women are better, and some possible explanation as to why. You may want to make yourself some popcorn and kick back, because this is going to take awhile.

THE RUNDOWN

For starters, women eat less meat. A lot less meat. While American women eat around 155 pounds of meat each year, men consume nearly 240 pounds—over 50 percent more meat per person. Male meat-eaters in the U.S. cause the suffering and death of about 37 farm animals each year, while women kill just 29 (USDA ERS, Commodity Consumption).

Women are also much more likely to be vegetarian. They outnumber male vegetarians at a roughly even pace all over the industrialized world, with studies documenting at least a two-to-one majority in the U.S., Canada, the United Kingdom, the Netherlands, and Australia. A study conducted across eleven different Eurasian countries found they outnumbered male vegetarians by a three-to-one ratio.

Women are also twice as likely as men to be semi-vegetarians (Vinnari *et al.* 2008; Rimal 2002; Humane Research Council, How Many Vegetarians). This is particularly significant given that semi-vegetarians are the main reason meat consumption in the U.S. has been dropping. The only black mark against women is they are slightly more likely to substitute chicken in their diet for red meat. Even so, they still eat far less chicken than men (USDA ERS, Commodity Consumption).

Studies conducted throughout Europe and the English-speaking world consistently show women to hold more pro-animal and pro-vegetarian attitudes than men. Women are more likely than men to: believe that being vegetarian helps animals; have trouble separating meat from the image of the living animal; be health-conscious; think that soy could be a healthful addition to their diet; think vegetarianism is cool; have a favorable view of vegetarians and vegans; believe that using animals for food cannot be morally justified; be disgusted by meat; believe that food should be produced in ways that minimize animal suffering; say they've altered their eating patterns for ethical or animal welfare reasons; express generally pro-animal attitudes; care for companion animals; oppose animal research; engage in grassroots animal advocacy; call a dissection choice hotline; go to animal-oriented summer camp; and join an animal protection organization (Ruby 2012; Worsley and Skrzypiec 1998; Lea, Moving From Meat; Rimal 2002; Lea and Worsley 2002; Beardsworth *et al.* 2002; Phillips *et al.* 2011; Herzog 2007; Bosman *et al.* 2009; Americans Pick Ronald McDonald; Kubberod 2005; Herzog and Golden 2009; Kubberod *et al.* 2008).

Women are less likely than men to believe that humans were made to eat meat, to believe that a healthful diet needs to include meat, to have pro-meat attitudes such as "I feel fit after eating meat," and to view the world in dog-eat-dog Darwinian terms (Ruby 2012; Lea and Worsley 2002; Kubberod *et al.* 2002; Kruse 1999).

All that being said, it's not as if the majority of women are knocking on the door of vegetarianism. The differences within each gender are much larger than the differences between each gender (Herzog 2007). There are huge numbers of animal-friendly men and plenty of vehemently pro-meat women. The trends shown here just represent the average results from each gender.

DO WOMEN RESPOND BETTER TO VEGETARIAN ADVOCACY EFFORTS?

Common sense would suggest that because women are more likely to be vegetarian and semi-vegetarian, and because they are much more pro-vegetarian than men, women are also more likely to respond positively to vegetarian advocacy. Some research and anecdotal evidence seem to bear that out.

In 2011, an investigation into the cruelty of the live export trade received widespread television coverage in Australia. Live export is the process of shipping living animals to slaughterhouses overseas. While live export is banned in some parts of the world, Australian farmers ship large numbers of animals each year to halal slaughterhouses in other countries.

Researchers polled the public to see what they thought of the story, and found women were more likely than men to have nearly every response animal advocates would want. Women were more likely to be sad or angry, to admire the investigators, to hate those involved with the cruelty, to be determined to stop live exports, to discuss the issue with others, and to perform some action in response—such as blogging about the issue, donating to the organizations that conducted the investigation, or giving up meat (Tiplady *et al.* 2012).

In the U.S., additional evidence suggests that women respond better to vegetarian advocacy. Among college students who decided to ditch meat after getting a leaflet from the group Vegan Outreach, women outnumber men by at least two to one (Grupe; Vegan Outreach). Online ads run by The Humane League brought teenagers to a website that showed a video on factory farming and offered them a free vegetarian starter pack. Women visitors were more than twice as likely to be inspired enough that they ordered a vegetarian starter pack (THL Ad Gender Comparisons). (In the interest of full disclosure, I am the founder of The Humane League.)

Women are also dramatically more likely to leave positive comments saying they plan to go vegetarian in response to online videos about factory farming. This holds true even after accounting for the fact that women are more likely than men to post Facebook comments in general (Netburn; Emerson; Goudreau).

None of these measurements are proof that women respond better to vegetarian advocacy than men, but it seems likely they do. The results are all in the same direction, and they closely match the gender breakdown of current vegetarians. So it appears that women aren't just twice as likely to be vegetarian, they're also twice as likely to go vegetarian when encouraged to do so.

Assuming that's true, what does it mean for vegetarian advocates? It means that targeting women should be twice as effective as targeting men. And it means that targeting women only should be about 33 percent more effective than targeting women and men equally. After you account for the fact that men eat more meat, targeting women should still spare about 20 percent more farm animals than targeting men and women equally.

To illustrate that difference, let's say a nonprofit's vegetarian advocacy was focused on men and women equally—in other words, the general public. Through their hard work they inspired ten people to go vegetarian. What a success! Thanks to their efforts, around 230 animals each year will be spared a lifetime of misery.

But what if, instead of targeting men and women equally, they had only targeted women? Instead of inspiring ten people to go vegetarian, they would have created thirteen. And instead of sparing around 230 animals each year, they would have spared 276. That's almost fifty more animals they would have spared just by focusing on women!

When we think about how valuable each individual animal is, sparing fifty extra lives is a big deal. Then consider the impact this would have on a national level. If vegetarian advocacy organizations focused most of their efforts on women, they could spare millions more animals from a life of misery—with little extra work.

The benefits of focusing on women may not stop there. Not only are women probably more likely to go vegetarian when encouraged to do so, they may also be more likely to inspire others to stop eating meat.

Women are more social and communicative than men, both online and offline (Netburn; Emerson; Goudreau). Because they're more likely to share information in general, they should also be more likely to share pro-vegetarian information. Whether through Facebook posts or handwritten recipes, women are probably more likely to share the realities of factory farming and the benefits of vegetarian eating with their friends and family. As a result, female vegetarians may be more likely than male vegetarians to inspire others to ditch meat.

And there's another reason women are more likely than men to influence what other people eat. In most households, they still buy and cook the food. A 2002 study found that women were five times more likely than men to say they decided what food to buy. They were also five times more likely to prepare the food, and three times more likely to do the bulk of the shopping (Beardsworth *et al.* 2002). Another study found that 80 percent of women were responsible for household purchasing decisions (McEachern 2005). Perhaps that's because a large portion of men still think buying, cooking, and serving food is a female activity (Ruby 2012). If these shopping and cooking trends hold true among vegetarians, they are yet another benefit of focusing vegetarian advocacy on women.

WHY IS THERE A GENDER DIFFERENCE IN THE FIRST PLACE?

Why is there such a big difference between men and women when it comes to meat?

For one thing, women and men have different values. One study showed that if you look at women and men who share the same values, women are only slightly more likely to be vegetarian (Kalof *et al.* 1999). This certainly isn't the only issue where different values lead men and women to make different choices. The past few Presidential elections have made clear that men and women want different things for themselves and society.

How do men's and women's values differ when it comes to vegetarian eating? As we saw earlier, women care much more about animals and animal welfare. They're also more likely to care about their health and weight, to know about nutrition, and to think a vegetarian diet is healthy (Rimal 2002; Ruby 2012; White *et al.* 1999). Men are more likely to cite health as a reason to eat meat than as a reason to avoid it (Rothberger 2012). Since health and animal welfare are the main reasons people go vegetarian, it's not surprising that women are more likely to make the switch.

Another factor is that meat-eating is seen as a masculine activity. Studies have shown that both vegetarians and omnivores think vegetarian men are less masculine than meat-eating men (Ruby 2012; Ruby and Heine 2011).

Some men will avoid anything that makes them look or feel less masculine. The more they value their perceived masculinity, the less likely they are to make a switch. One study of middle-aged men found that carpenters, who may be considered stereotypically masculine, both favored meat and embraced masculine ideals more than engineers (who may be thought of as less stereotypically masculine). (Rothberger 2012) Another study revealed that people who endorsed masculine values—whether men or women—were more likely to eat beef, pork, and chicken, and less likely to eat vegetarian meals. These masculine values included the beliefs that men should not show pain and that they should be emotionally restricted, athletic, and dominant (Rothberger 2012).

If advocates of vegetarian eating ever focus our efforts on men, they may want to address the perceptions that prevent men from ditching meat. First, they need to show men that meat is unhealthful. Connecting meat with male-specific health issues like prostate cancer might be helpful. Second, they need to counteract the perception that eating vegetarian food makes you less masculine. Researchers suggest that vegetarian advocates may want to use images of muscular men, or messages that could fit in with masculine norms like "be your own man" or "take control of your health" (Rothberger 2012). The unfortunate reality is that when it comes to persuading men to go vegetarian, lack of information is not the only barrier. Gender norms are also a major hindrance, and should be addressed.

JUSTIFYING MEAT-EATING: MEN VS. WOMEN

There's one more difference between men and women on this issue. According to one study, women have a different strategy than men for preventing the guilty feelings that can come from eating meat.

Because men care less about animals, they have no problem justifying their decision to eat meat. Men are more likely to endorse pro-meat attitudes and to deny that animals suffer. They're also more likely to use hierarchical (we're the top of the food chain), religious (a god gave us permission to eat animals), health (you need meat to be healthy), and human destiny/fate (it's just how things are) justifications for eating meat. Because women care more about animals, they're less willing to directly rationalize eating meat. Instead they try to avoid thinking about it, or to mentally separate meat from the animal it came from.

People who eat more meat, whether male or female, tend to use the male strategy. Those who eat less meat tend to adopt the female approach. It's hard to know whether the behavior or the attitude came first here. People who eat a lot of meat may need stronger justifications for their actions, which could cause them to use the head-on male strategy. On the other hand, they may eat more meat as a result of having those attitudes. In either case, people seem to exist on a continuum of eating a lot of meat and explicitly justifying it, to eating less meat and trying to avoid thinking about it, to not eating meat at all (and feeling great about it).

Interestingly, fish consumption didn't fit in with the general trend. People who were somewhat uncomfortable with eating meat, and who tried to avoid thinking about it, didn't have the same qualms about eating fish. They didn't need to justify or avoid thinking about their fish consumption because it didn't bother them. This is probably because, as we'll discuss further in Chapter 12, humans have less empathy for fish than other animals (Harrison 2010; Westbury and Neumann 2008).

AN EQUAL WORLD

There's one last thing worth noting about gender and meat consumption. In Chapter 10 we'll see that people who live in more economically equal countries tend to eat less meat. In a similar vein, countries with more gender equality also seem to provide better outcomes for animals. A survey of eleven Eurasian countries found that women in more gender-equal countries, and also those in more gender-equal households, cared more about animals (Phillips *et al.* 2011). A study of a hundred non-technological cultures found that the most patriarchal ones, where women had the least power and performed gender-specific work, also ate the most meat. Plant-based societies were the most egalitarian (Sanday).

A more gender-equal world seems to go hand in hand with a kinder world for animals.

6

MAKING THE SWITCH

HOW PEOPLE GO VEGETARIAN

WHAT DOES THE TRANSITION FROM MEAT-EATER TO VEG-etarian look like? A handful of studies have taken a quantitative look at how people make the switch. Here's what they found.

THE POINT OF CHANGE

People rarely alter their behavior overnight. They usually need to hear an idea a number of times before actually making a change. The same probably goes for vegetarian eating. Nonetheless, usually one event or experience tips the scales and launches people into the world of meat-free living. So, what is it?

In one survey, about a third of vegetarians made the switch after seeing some form of media: a book, pamphlet, TV show, radio show, or speaker. Another third went vegetarian from the influence of a friend, family member, or group; 13 percent switched after learning information that wasn't intended to make them go vegetarian; 9 percent switched after witnessing cruelty; and 8 percent changed due to a health emergency (MacNair 1998).

This survey was done before YouTube, Facebook, and the social media revolution came into existence. What's causing people to go vegetarian today might be very different, especially among young people. The Internet may be the new star of the show. A 2010 meat industry survey found that early adopters—people who make changes before the rest of society—look to the Internet first for information about the food system. Family, friends, and television now trail behind (New Research Shows).

A 2009 survey, carried out at a vegetarian food festival, found the main inspirations for going vegetarian to be: "my own inner voice," 24 percent; friend or family member, 18 percent; video or photo, 15 percent; encounter with an animal, 10 percent; brochure, magazine, or non-fiction book, 9 percent; discussion with others, 3 percent; doctor's advice, 2 percent; and 7 percent in the lumped category "spiritual/ religious/born vegetarian." Vegans were inspired in similar ways, except they cited brochures, magazines, and non-fiction books more often (Chlebowski).

At what point in their lives are people going vegetarian? Not surprisingly, a large percentage of conversions seem to happen between the ages of thirteen and twenty-five.

A study of people who were vegetarian at age nineteen found that they had, on average, ditched meat six years earlier (Forestell *et al.* 2012). A study of people who were vegetarian at age thirty found that a third of them were already meat-free by sixteen, and the majority switched between adolescence and their early twenties (Gale *et al.* 2007). A series of focus groups found that most vegetarians had made the switch in their late teens to mid-twenties (Humane Research Council, Focus Groups). A study of vegetarian Croats, with an average age of thirty-six, found the average age at which respondents went vegetarian was twenty-four. The study also found that men and women went vegetarian at about the same age (Bobic *et al.* 2012).

One thing these studies can't tell us is at what age successful vegetarians—those who never go back to eating meat—tend to make the switch. To do that, researchers would need to survey only vegetarians who are at the end of their life. And even if they did, the results might not apply to the current generation; eating vegetarian is much easier now, so the success rate may be higher. The success rate could also be lower if many people are trying out vegetarianism, since it's trendy, but quickly abandoning it.

EASY DOES IT

Even after they've decided to go vegetarian, most people make the transition gradually. For some it is very, very gradual.

One survey found that 23 percent of vegetarians had made a slow, gradual transition. Another 30 percent had already been cutting down on meat but then suddenly cut out the remainder. Just one in five vegetarians had gone from full-fledged meat-eater to vegetarian overnight (MacNair 1998). Several other studies have found almost identical results (MacNair 2001; Powell 2002; Stiles 1998).

One smaller study did find that two-thirds of vegetarians had gone from meat-eater to vegetarian overnight (Boyle 2011). The average age of people in this study was a bit lower than others, so it's possible that young people are more likely to make an abrupt switch.

For people who make the change gradually, how long does the transition usually last? One study indicated people typically took between six months and three years to phase meat out of their diet (MacNair 2001). Another survey, which looked at the switch in closer detail, found that 22 percent changed in six months or less, 16 percent took six months to a year, 26 percent took one to two years, 14 percent took two to three years, and 23 percent took more than three years to make the transition. Put more simply, about two-thirds of gradual vegetarians made the switch within two years (MacNair 1998).

Some groups tend to stop more abruptly than others. One study discovered that 31 percent of vegans had ceased eating meat overnight, compared to 22 percent of vegetarians. And 38 percent of those whose primary motivation was helping animals stopped suddenly, compared to 22 percent of vegetarians overall (MacNair 1998). Another study confirmed that vegans and people motivated by animal welfare concerns were most likely to halt abruptly. Those motivated by environmental concerns were least likely to make a sudden switch (Haverstock and Forgays 2012). If young people really are more likely to go vegetarian overnight—as one study suggested—maybe it's because they tend to be motivated by animal welfare concerns (Boyle 2011).

Whether they switch gradually or abruptly, what does a new vegetarian's diet look like? One study found that two-thirds of vegetarians begin as lacto-ovo vegetarians: they eat dairy and eggs, but not meat. The remaining third started as pescatarians, lacto-vegetarians, or vegans.

Even most vegans start off as vegetarians. One study found that two-thirds of vegans start off as vegetarians (MacNair 1998). Another study showed four out of every five vegans was a vegetarian first. And the change wasn't quick: it took them an average of six years before they removed eggs and dairy from their diet (Hirschler 2011). Why does it take vegetarians so long to go vegan? One study found that most vegetarians see a vegan diet as difficult and potentially unhealthful (Povey *et al.* 2001).

HOW IT FEELS

A lot of new vegetarians transition alone, but not as many as we might have guessed. One study found that just half of all new vegetarians went through the process without moral support from their friends or family. Meanwhile, 18 percent said others were interested in their switch, 18 percent were brought to it by friends or family members, and 7 percent made the transition along with someone else, usually a spouse or family member (MacNair 1998).

How did it feel to break up with meat? In one study, a third of vegetarians said the decision was motivated by emotions. One out of every four said it was purely a logical decision. One out of every ten felt tired of being a hypocrite, and—in heart-warming news—13 percent said they used to be hostile to vegetarianism and had argued against it (MacNair 1998). So don't give up hope on that co-worker of yours who likes to make fun of your vegan lunches!

Interestingly, one study discovered that women who went vegetarian reported receiving more hostility from friends and family than men did. That hostility typically came from men (Merriman 2010). This may be a bit of surprise. Meat is linked more with masculinity than femininity, so a woman shunning meat should be seen as less unusual than a man doing the same.

Do new vegetarians miss meat? Initially they do, but the feeling fades with time. One study showed that those who missed the taste of meat had been vegetarian an average of only three years. Those who didn't miss meat, or who were actively repulsed by it, had been vegetarian an average of eleven years (MacNair 1998). So our tastes do change. Unfortunately, that change can seem glacially slow to new vegetarians. One study of former vegetarians found that almost 20 percent had gone back to meat because they missed the taste of it too much (Herzog, Why Do Most Vegetarians).

VEGETARIANS OVER TIME

Sadly, most vegetarians eventually go back to eating meat. At least 75 percent of self-defined vegetarians will one day resume their omnivorous ways. In Chapter 9 we'll look at who these former vegetarians are and why they went back to eating meat.

During the period people *are* vegetarian, though—whether for a few years or a lifetime—they tend to become stricter (Rozin *et al.* 1997). One study tracked vegetarian college women over the course of a year. Of those who stayed vegetarian, 14 percent became more restrictive of animal products. Among those who had been semi-vegetarian, a year later 37 percent had adopted some form of vegetarian-ism (Forestell *et al.* 2012). A wider study found that nearly two-thirds of current vegetarians or vegans had adopted stricter diets over time. Only 10 percent now ate more animal products than when they first began identifying as a vegetarian (Barr and Chapman 2002).

7

WHY THEY DO IT

THE REAL REASONS PEOPLE DITCH MEAT

SO FAR WE'VE LOOKED AT WHAT KIND OF PEOPLE GO
vegetarian and how they make the switch. What we haven't looked at yet is why
they do it. Why do people decide to give up meat?

Browse through a vegetarian advocacy website and you'll see a laundry list of motivations to go meat-free. You'll read that going vegetarian is good for your health, that
it spares animals from a lifetime of cruelty, and that it's good for the environment. You
might read that it helps fight global starvation, or see religious or spiritual impulses to
make the switch.

The list of reasons grows much longer once you get into the details. Going vegetarian will save the rain forest, lower air pollution, stop water pollution, feed more people,
save water, spare animals from misery, mitigate the effects of climate change, avoid
antibiotic overuse, prevent heart disease, fight cancer, cut down on obesity, reverse
diabetes, and on and on. The list seems endless.

But what is *actually* motivating people to make the switch? Is there one key issue
that really inspires people? If there were, advocates of vegetarian eating would probably want to focus on that issue. Doing so should resonate with more people, and inspire more to change their diet.

THE REASON WHY

If we look at individual studies on why people go vegetarian, the results can vary dramatically. In some, health is far and away the main motivation for going vegetarian. In
others, concern for animals is the runaway champion. It's hard to tell which edges out
the other as the top impetus. What is clear is that most people go vegetarian to improve
their health or to protect animals from cruelty. No other motivations come close.

A lot of surveys ask people why they went vegetarian. Here are the results from some of the most representative and reliable of them.

MOTIVATION STUDY 1

Health	Animals	Religion	Environment	World Hunger
50%	21%	6%	4%	1%

This representative national 2002 U.S. phone survey, conducted by Time/CNN, polled 400 actual vegetarians. The study accurately defined vegetarians and excluded semi-vegetarians. The Health group breaks down into the following specific motivations: Health (32 percent), Antibiotics (15 percent), and Weight (3 percent). The Animals group breaks down into the following: Love of Animals (11 percent) and Animal Rights (10 percent) (Humane Research Council, Why or Why Not Vegetarian; Time/CNN Poll).

MOTIVATION STUDY 2

Ethics	Health	Environment	Religion
67%	20%	9%	3%

This 2012 U.S. written survey polled 145 people. The majority of respondents were 18–25, and the average age in the study was 26, so this group is younger than the population as a whole. The study accurately defined vegetarians and excluded semi-vegetarians. It measured people's initial and current reason for being vegetarian, and found the two were almost identical. The survey was carried out in two large cities and online. The Health group breaks down into the following: Health (17 percent) and Weight (3 percent) (Timko *et al.* 2012).

MOTIVATION STUDY 3

Animals	Health	Environment	Taste	Religion
30%	28%	10%	10%	8%

This representative national 2005 U.S. online survey polled about forty actual vegetarians and excluded semi-vegetarians. The average age in this study was slightly younger than in the population as a whole. The Health group breaks down into the following: Health (20 percent); Cancer/Diabetes (5 percent); Weight (3 percent) (Humane Research Council, Why or Why Not Vegetarian; Humane Research Council, Appendix).

MOTIVATION STUDY 4

Health	Animals	Environment	Religion
78%	10%	9%	3%

This international 2011 survey polled a hundred European and Asian college students who were vegetarian. Nearly all of those polled were actual vegetarians and not semi-vegetarians (Izmirli and Phillips 2011).

Most of the other studies that look at why people go vegetarian are not representative. In other words, the vegetarians who are being measured are a somewhat unique group of people. They may all live in the same city, or many of them may be friends with one another. Therefore, the results of these studies wouldn't necessarily apply to vegetarians overall.

For what it's worth, these non-representative polls tend to have similar results to the representative ones. For example, here's what a few of them found:

MOTIVATION STUDY 5

Animals	Health	Animals & Health Equally	Taste
40%	23%	14%	12%

This 2006 British study carried out in-person interviews with forty-three people, ten of whom were actually pescatarian (Hamilton, Eating Death).

MOTIVATION STUDY 6

Become a Better Person (physically, mentally, spiritually)	Animals	Taste	Social Pressure	Social Justice
50%	40%	31%	9%	4%

This 2011 American study carried out in-person interviews with forty-five self-defined vegetarians. The respondents were younger than the population as a whole, with many being college students. Respondents were allowed to pick more than one main motivation, though most picked only one (Boyle 2011).

MOTIVATION STUDY 7

Ethics	Health	Taste	Environment
57%	17%	12%	1%

This 1989 British survey carried out in-person interviews with seventy-six self-described vegetarians. Out of these eighteen turned out to be pescatarians, and five still ate some meat (Beardsworth and Kiel 1992).

WHETHER WE JUST look at the representative surveys or we look at all of the surveys, we see the same results: to improve their health and to help animals are the two main reasons people go vegetarian. Concern for the environment, a dislike of the taste of meat, and religious motivation all trail well behind, each inspiring fewer than 10 percent of vegetarians. And concern for social justice or world hunger is almost never the reason people go vegetarian.

HEALTH VEGETARIANS AND ETHICAL VEGETARIANS: BROTHERS FROM ANOTHER MOTHER

While they share a common diet, there are some differences between people who go vegetarian for ethical reasons (usually to protect animals) and people who go vegetarian for their health.

For one thing, meat is a bigger deal to ethical vegetarians. They find meat more disgusting, have stronger emotional reactions to it, and are more bothered by other people eating it. They are also more likely to think that eating meat can alter someone's personality. And while health vegetarians don't get upset when they accidentally eat meat, ethical vegetarians do. Those who have gotten a mouthful of meat said they felt anxious, angry, guilty, contaminated, uneasy, queasy, and revolted afterwards (Rozin et al. 1997; Ruby 2012; MacNair 1998).

As a result, if you ask an ethical vegetarian why they've made the switch they'll probably tell you about the negative aspects of meat. Health vegetarians, on the other hand, are more likely to focus on how good vegetarian food can be. Ethical vegetarians are more likely to cite emotional reasons for going meat-free, while health vegetarians say their decision was based on logic (MacNair 1998; MacNair 2001). One thing that health and ethical vegetarians seem to have in common is that they know the same amount about vegetarian nutrition (Hoffman et al. 2013).

Ethical vegetarians are more disgusted by meat than health vegetarians and the general public. But that's not because they are more squeamish overall. When it comes to other potentially disgusting things, like dead human bodies or rotting food, ethical vegetarians experience the same level of disgust as everyone else; their disgust toward meat sets in only after they've gone vegetarian. It's their ethical beliefs about meat, and their awareness of what it is and how it was produced, that cause them to be so revolted by meat and its sensory properties (Fessler et al. 2003; Hamilton, Eating Death).

One study compared the personalities of health vegetarians and ethical vegetarians. The only significant difference the study revealed was that health vegetarians tended to be more extroverted (Bobic et al. 2012). A second study looked at the social beliefs of each group. It found that both were more opposed to nuclear war and capital punishment, and more were supportive of abortion and environmental organizations, than omnivores. However, ethical vegetarians held each of these beliefs more strongly than health vegetarians (Hamilton 2000). Another study found that ethical vegetarians were a bit more likely to have earned a bachelor's or graduate degree (Hoffman et al. 2013).

Ethical vegetarians may feel more strongly about their diet than health vegetarians. One study showed they were more likely to—among other things—encourage people to go vegetarian, believe everyone should stop eating meat, and see vegetarianism as part of who they were. The differences weren't large though. Their agreement with each of these statements was only 5–8 percent higher than it was for health vegetarians. And much of the difference disappeared once you factored in how long they'd been vegetarian (Hoffman et al. 2013).

Ethical vegetarians seem much more likely to stick with their initial motivation. In one study 92 percent of them kept ethics as their main reason for being meat-free, while 6 percent stayed vegetarian for health reasons. Those who had initially ditched meat for health reasons were far more likely to adopt a new motivation. A quarter of them were now vegetarian primarily for ethical reasons (Hoffman et al. 2013).

Do ethical vegetarians do a better job at being meat-free than health vegetarians?

One study from the 1990s found that ethical vegetarians and semi-vegetarians (lumped together into one group) avoided a wider range of animal products than those motivated by health (Rozin et al. 1997). Another study discovered that, among female physicians in the U.S. who identified as vegetarian, those whose diet was motivated by health ate slightly more fish than those motivated by other reasons. And those who were trying to lose weight ate more poultry and fish than those not motivated by weight concerns (White et al. 1999).

On the other hand, a study of vegetarian medical-school students suggested that those who cited health as one of their motivations ate meat less often than students who didn't. Unfortunately this study only looked at overall meat consumption; it didn't differentiate between red meat, poultry, and fish (Spencer et al. 2007). Another study indicated that people who initially stopped eating meat for health reasons were just as likely to go vegan as those who had ditched it for ethical reasons (Hoffman et al. 2013).

Although these studies are interesting, none gives us a reliable answer to our question. Two are focused on a very unique community—people in the medical profession—and have contradictory results. A third examines the number of animal products avoided, not the quantity of meat that's eaten. The last study looks only at the likelihood of going vegan, not how much meat vegetarians eat.

For what it's worth, one of these studies also found ethically motivated vegetarians and semi-vegetarians had a larger number of reasons for continuing to avoid meat. In theory, that could make them more likely to stay vegetarian. The researchers also speculate that ethical vegetarians might be more successful at handing their eating habits down to their children, since values are easier to pass on than preferences (Rozin et al. 1997).

Moving on, a recent study found that ethical vegetarians make the transition to meat-free eating more quickly (Fox and Ward 2008). This sounds like a good thing until we consider the fact that people who go vegetarian abruptly are more likely to go back to eating meat than those who switch gradually (Haverstock and Forgays 2012).

As for whether ethical or health vegetarians are more likely to backslide, the data aren't very clear. One study suggested that current vegetarians care a lot more about animal welfare, and only slightly more about their health, than former vegetarians (Haverstock and Forgays 2012). This could imply that caring about animals is important for sticking with a meat-free diet, but it ain't necessarily so.

Regardless of how much they cared about animals when they were vegetarian, people who have gone back to eating meat will be likely to say they care less about animals. If they didn't, their beliefs would be out of line with their behavior. Psychologists call this kind of uncomfortable realization "cognitive dissonance." People try to avoid it by adjusting their stated beliefs to match their behavior. In this case, cognitive dissonance should cause former vegetarians to say they care less about animals.

Only one real survey has been conducted to see how different types of vegetarians stick with their diet. Between 2006 and 2009, *Vegetarian Journal* magazine tracked 150 of its readers to see how many of them stayed meat-free. Over the course of three years, 91 percent of those who had gone vegetarian for health reasons remained vegetarian. That compares to 92 percent of those motivated by animal rights, and 94 percent motivated by "ethics" (Stahler, Retention Survey). So there appears to be, at least in this one survey, very little short-term difference between health and ethical vegetarians when it comes to sticking with cruelty-free cuisine.

Here's the bottom line: There are a few real differences between ethical vegetarians and health vegetarians in how they feel about meat. But the data don't suggest that one group is dramatically better than the other in terms of the overall impact they have on farm animals.

VEGETARIANS YOUNG AND OLD: DIFFERING MOTIVATIONS

Not only are young people much more likely than other age groups to go vegetarian, they also have different reasons for doing it. Young vegetarians are more likely to be motivated by animal welfare concerns and less likely to be motivated by worries over their health.

One recent study looked at six- to ten-year-old children who were vegetarians. Of the sixteen kids who had gone vegetarian on their own, every single one had done so because they cared about animals. A few also didn't like the taste of meat, and one was also motivated by health (Hussar and Harris 2010).

Teenage vegetarians are also more likely than older vegetarians to cite animal welfare or environmental reasons for ditching meat (The TRU Study; Pribis et al. 2010; Timko et al. 2012; Beardsworth and Bryman 1999). One study showed that, in addition to animal welfare concerns, feelings of disgust toward meat and social pressures were important motivators (Humane Research Council, Why or Why Not Vegetarian).

Health concerns seem to take over as the primary reason for going vegetarian once people reach their late forties (MacNair 1998). A large 2012 U.S. study found that while almost two-thirds of older vegetarians said health was one of their reasons for avoiding meat, only about a third of young vegetarians said the same (Haverstock and Forgays 2012).

Only one study concluded that health concerns were almost as important as animals for teenage vegetarians (Perry et al. 2001). That study also revealed something else surprising: weight control was a major motivator among respondents. Surveys of vegetarian college students and adults have usually found that only around 3 percent are motivated by a desire to manage their weight (Humane Research Council, Why or Why Not Vegetarian; Timko et al. 2012; Humane Research Council, Appendix; Curtis and Comer 2006). In this one survey of eleven- to eighteen-year-olds, about one in five said the main reason they ditched meat was to lose the pounds (Perry et al. 2001).

The fact that young vegetarians care more about animals and the environment, and less about health, has an interesting implication: ethical vegetarians are probably more likely than health vegetarians to be actual vegetarians. Why? Because health vegetarians tend to be older, and older people are more likely to inaccurately identify themselves as vegetarian. Ethical vegetarians tend to be younger, and younger people are much more accurate in defining themselves as vegetarians.

We have to keep in mind here that it's not the motivation that matters, it's the person's age. As far as we know, a teenage health vegetarian and a teenage ethical vegetarian are equally likely to be truly meat-free.

WHY VEGANS DO IT

Like young people, vegans are more likely to be prompted by a concern for animals. They might also be more likely to be induced to change by a concern for the environment.

A 1998 study found that vegans were twice as likely as vegetarians to cite concern for animals as their main impetus (MacNair 1998). An online poll conducted the same year found similar results: while vegetarians were more likely to be motivated by health concerns, vegans were more likely to be concerned about animals (Consumers Prefer Meat-Free). Several other studies have also found that vegans are more likely than vegetarians to be motivated by animal ethics (Humane Research Council, Why or Why Not Vegetarian; Stahler, Sugar).

A 2012 study revealed that vegans were more concerned than vegetarians with the animal welfare, environmental, and political issues surrounding food choices. They had the same amount of concern when it came to personal health (Haverstock and Forgays 2012).

THE CHANGING MOTIVATIONS OF VEGETARIANS

While the data are mixed, some surveys have found that vegetarians add, drop, and change their motivations for remaining meat-free.

One small-scale study found that three-quarters of vegetarians surveyed had altered their motivations in some way since first ditching meat. One-third had added motives, a quarter had both added and dropped motives, and 15 percent had simply dropped a motive (Hamilton, Eating Death). One study noted that health, ethical, and other vegetarians incorporated new motives at an equal rate (Stiles 1998). On the other hand, a study of 145 vegetarians and vegans observed that fewer than 5 percent had changed their main motivation at all. This was the case despite the fact that they'd been vegan or vegetarian for an average of eight years (Timko et al. 2012).

When it comes to primary motivations, ethical vegetarians are more likely to stick with their initial reason. In one study only 8 percent of them later changed their primary motivation, compared to 38 percent of health vegetarians and 75 percent of other vegetarians (Hoffman et al. 2013).

"Other" vegetarians—those not initially motivated by health or ethics—are most likely to change their main motivation. One study indicated that three-quarters of the number of people who stopped eating meat for taste reasons, or because their friends or family were vegetarian, stuck with it for other reasons. The majority remained vegetarian over ethical concerns, though some cited health (Hoffman et al. 2013) as an impulse. Three studies found that many health vegetarians went on to adopt animal welfare or environmental reasons for avoiding meat (Hamilton, Eating Death; Hamilton, Disgust Reactions; Fox and Ward 2008; Hoffman et al. 2013). In one study, a full 25 percent of those who had ditched meat for their health stuck with their diet mainly for ethical reasons (Hoffman et al. 2013).

But it's not just health vegetarians who are adding or changing their motivations. Some ethical vegetarians stopped believing eating meat was unethical, but continued to be vegetarian for health reasons. Others lost the taste for meat or simply stayed vegetarian out of habit. Many ethical vegetarians later added health as an additional reason to remain meat-free (Rozin et al. 1997; Hamilton, Eating Death; Hamilton, Disgust Reactions; Hoffman et al. 2013). One study discovered that, regardless of the reason people initially went vegetarian, a number of them became motivated by health as they aged (Hoffman et al. 2013).

Another study found a lot of vegetarians adding green concerns. Although few people went vegetarian over worries about detrimental effects on the environment, many vegetarians eventually added that as a reason for staying meat-free (Fox and Ward 2008). Other studies back this up. Only a small number of people cite the environment as their main reason for ditching meat, but polls show up to 47 percent including it as one of their reasons for staying vegetarian (Humane Research Council, Why or Why Not Vegetarian; Timko et al. 2012; Humane Research Council, Appendix; Beardsworth and Keil 1992).

Adding other motivations makes sense from a psychological perspective. As discussed earlier, people often shift their beliefs so that they line up with their behavior. Once someone is a vegetarian, even if it's for health reasons, it's much easier for them to adopt the belief that farms are cruel toward animals, or that vegetarian eating is good for the planet. For one thing, those are beliefs that make sense given your behavior. And second, since you're not eating meat, you can accept those ideas without feeling like you're a bad person.

If vegetarians do tend to pile on the motivations over time, that's probably a good thing. Having extra motives should help people strengthen their conviction and stick with a meat-free diet (Humane Research Council, Why or Why Not Vegetarian).

SECONDARY REASONS FOR GOING VEGETARIAN

When we're looking at people's additional reasons for being vegetarian, we have to be careful. If people are allowed to choose multiple reasons for why they're meat-free, it's easy for them to check off a whole laundry list of causes. One or two of these were the important motivations, the ones that actually got them to switch. The rest are a bonus but weren't vital to their decision. If we're not careful, we can get confused about what actually inspires people to go vegetarian.

For example, a 2008 study of *Vegetarian Times* readers asked people to choose all of the reasons they were vegetarian. The top three answers' percentages—animal welfare (54 percent), health (53 percent), and environmental concerns (47 percent)—are so close that it appears that each is equally important in getting people to ditch meat. As we saw earlier, however, that's not the case. When you ask people the primary reason they went vegetarian, concern for the environment never gets above 10 percent. It motivates far fewer people than concern for animals or health (Humane Research Council, Why or Not Vegetarian).

Here's another example. A 2005 U.S. poll asked people to list all of the reasons they were vegetarian. Their top picks were: health (65 percent), animal welfare (55 percent), environment (30 percent), avoiding antibiotics/additives (30 percent), reducing fat and cholesterol intake (28 percent), and taste (23 percent). When the study then asked people what their main motivation was, the results shifted significantly. Animal welfare jumped to the top of the list with 30 percent, followed by health (20 percent), with environment (10 percent) and taste (10 percent) trailing. Avoiding antibiotics and reducing fat and cholesterol, which seemed like important issues based on the first question, dropped to zero. Not a single person had gone vegetarian for those reasons. Meanwhile, other health concerns climbed the charts—such as worry about cancer and diabetes, which registered at 5 percent (Humane Research Council, Why Or Why Not Vegetarian).

It's nice to know some of the side issues that make people happy to be vegetarians. But vegetarian advocates should look for guidance to studies showing people's primary motivation for switching. These should indicate which messages are most likely to persuade people to make a change.

SEMI-VEGETARIANS: WHY THEY DO IT

Semi-vegetarians are wholly different beasts from vegetarians. In some ways, their personalities and lifestyle choices fall at the midway point between vegetarians and omnivores. In other ways, they lean much closer toward omnivores than they do toward vegetarians (Baker et al. 2002).

The difference between semi-vegetarians and vegetarians is particularly pronounced when it comes to why they leave meat off their plate. Among vegetarians, health and animal welfare concerns go head to head as the top motivations. For semi-vegetarians, most studies have found health to be far and away the biggest motivation. No other issue even comes close. This is true both for semi-vegetarians who cut back on the total amount of animal flesh they eat, and for those who stop eating certain types, such as red meat (Latvala et al., Humane Research Council, Appendix; Perry et al. 2001; Timko et al. 2012; Curtis and Comer 2006; Tobler et al. 2011; Lea et al. 2006; Barclay; Focus Groups for the Johns Hopkins Pilot; Mooney and Walbourn 2001; AllRecipes).

Here are the results of the most reliable study on what motivates semi-vegetarians who are cutting back on meat.

MOTIVATION STUDY 8

Health	Money	Taste	Animals	Religion	Environment
74%	10%	3%	2%	1%	0%

This representative 2005 U.S. survey collected answers from around a thousand people who said they had cut back on meat over the past year. Meat was defined as including red meat, chicken, and fish. Some respondents may have only been reducing one type of meat, others may have been reducing all types. The Health group breaks down into the following: Healthier Diet (34 percent), Reduce Fat and Cholesterol (22 percent), Lose Weight (14 percent), Cancer/Diabetes (3 percent), and Antibiotics (1 percent) (Humane Research Council, Appendix).

These next two studies are the most reliable ones on people's motivations for cutting out red meat entirely, with some respondents also cutting back on poultry and fish.

MOTIVATION STUDY 9

Health	Animals	Religion
61%	19%	8%

This 2001 U.S. survey collected responses from 160 adolescent semi-vegetarians, aged 11–18, from the Minneapolis area. In this study, people who did not eat red meat but ate either chicken or fish were classified as semi-vegetarians. The Health group breaks down into the following: Weight (40 percent) and Health (21 percent) (Perry et al. 2001).

MOTIVATION STUDY 10

Ethics	Health	Environment	Religion
39%	35%	15%	6%

This 2012 U.S. survey covered 145 semi-vegetarians. The majority of participants were 18–25, with the average age in the study being 26. People who did not eat red meat but who did eat either chicken or fish were classified as semi-vegetarians. The Health group breaks down into the following: Health (28 percent) and Weight (7 percent) (Timko et al. 2012).

*　　*　　*

IS THERE A difference between semi-vegetarians who cut back on red meat and those who cut back on all types of meat? A large-scale 2011 Finnish survey found that the biggest difference was concern for animals and the environment. People who were eating less of all types of meat reported about 50 percent more concern for how their food choices impacted animals and the environment (Latvala *et al.*).

A 2003 American survey found similar results. Among semi-vegetarians who avoided certain types of meat, those who were primarily motivated by ethics or the environment ate 35 percent fewer servings of chicken per week than those whose primary motivation was health or taste. They also ate less red meat (Fessler *et al.* 2003).

So while semi-vegetarians are usually motivated by health, getting them to care more about animals or the environment could help them cut out not just red meat but all types of meat.

We need to keep in mind, though, that caring about animals and the environment doesn't automatically lead people to eat lower amounts of fish and poultry. A number of people with concern for animal welfare cut out or cut back on red meat and stop there (Latvala *et al.*). A 2012 U.S. survey of people who were consuming less red meat found that, although 66 percent cited health and 47 percent cited cost as a reason for cutting back, 30 percent cited animals and 29 percent cited the environment. Of course, since the study allowed people to list all of their reasons for cutting back, including their less important motivations, it's quite possible that animals and the environment weren't as much of a factor in their decision as these numbers suggest (Barclay).

The bottom line is this. People who care a lot about animals and the environment, in addition to health, seem more likely to cut down on all types of meat and not just red meat. So advocates of vegetarian eating may want to avoid advocacy materials that focus only on the health reasons for curbing meat consumption. Pairing the health reasons with the animal welfare reasons for cutting back on meat should do more good.

Still, let's not miss the forest for the trees. Health concerns are far and away the main reason that semi-vegetarians are cutting back on meat. Nothing else comes close in importance. So advocates who want to inspire more people to cut back on meat should be emphasizing the health benefits of doing so.

While the surveys on motivation make that clear, there are still more studies that back up the importance of the health message. A 2011 Swiss study showed that, while environmental and animal concerns led some people to consider eating less meat, another motive was needed to get them to actually follow through and make the change (Tobler *et al.* 2011). A 2006 Australian study found that most people didn't perceive major environmental or animal benefits to eating a reduced-meat diet (Lea *et al.* 2006).

In Chapter 14, we'll take a more in-depth look at which messages are most likely to inspire people to ditch meat.

8

BARRIERS

WHY PEOPLE AREN'T GOING VEGETARIAN
(ACCORDING TO THEM)

THOSE WHO HAVE CUT OUT MEAT KNOW THAT BEING VEG-
etarian is basically the greatest thing in the world. So why is it that many people don't
get it? Or, if they get it, why aren't more of them making the switch themselves?

Getting someone to make a switch isn't just a matter of showing them the benefits
of changing. It's also a matter of taking down any barriers that are in their way, whether
those barriers are real or imagined.

The main reasons people keep eating meat—or keep doing anything—are those
they aren't really conscious of. Eating meat is a habit, and habits are hard to break.
Most people don't want to put in the effort of learning how to eat a different way. They
also tend to automatically prefer the status quo. Most people's friends and family eat
meat, so there are strong social norms to do the same (Cooney 2011).

But people also have more surface-level reasons for sticking with meat. These are
the reasons they'll give if you ask them why they haven't gone vegetarian. Some may
be actual concerns; others may be little more than justifications. In either case, the
more we can address their reasons for remaining omnivores the more likely they'll be
to make a change.

THE FOUR BIG ONES

Numerous surveys in the U.S. and Europe have asked meat-eaters why they don't go
vegetarian. While the results vary survey to survey, when looked at as a whole, themes
emerge very clearly. People cite four main barriers for why they're sticking with meat.
Interestingly, they are almost identical to the reasons former vegetarians give for going
back to meat.

Taste is the biggest reason people don't go vegetarian. Meat-eaters love the taste of meat, and they don't want to give it up. They also worry that vegetarian food will taste bad, that a vegetarian diet is boring and not satisfying, and that they'll be missing out on their most cherished foods.

Health concerns are the other main reason people don't go vegetarian. Not everyone is aware that cutting out meat can have health benefits. Some see vegetarianism as a healthier way to eat, even though they might not be willing to make the switch. Others think vegetarian eating involves serious health risks. Their main concerns are that they won't be getting enough protein and iron, or will experience a general nutritional deficiency. Worries about protein are particularly strong among college students.

Next up are concerns that vegetarian eating is inconvenient. In a couple of surveys this ranked as the main reason people weren't going vegetarian, particularly among college students. People feel like they don't know how to make the switch to meat-free eating. They think vegetarian food is expensive, difficult to find, and time-consuming to prepare.

While it's far less important than the first three reasons, social anxieties about ditching meat mattered to people in a couple of studies. Some worried it would be hard to be vegetarian because their family eats meat, others that they'd feel isolated from their friends, or that their friends might think they were weird (Schosler *et al.* 2012; Lea and Worsley 2001; Beardsworth and Bryman 2004; Ketchum; Humane Research Council, Focus Groups; Lea, Moving From Meat; Rimal 2002; Lea and Worsley, 2003; Lea and Worsley 2002; Hirschler 2011; Humane Research Council, Why or Why Not Vegetarian; Wyker and Davison 2010; Stiles 1998).

OTHER BARRIERS

Children who want to go vegetarian have an extra barrier to hurdle: their parents. Why is it that many parents don't want their kids to give up meat? Health and convenience are their main concerns. They worry that a vegetarian diet isn't healthful, and they don't want the hassle of having to buy and prepare separate vegetarian meals (Humane Research Council, Why or Why Not Vegetarian).

Semi-vegetarians have it much easier. People thinking about cutting back on meat don't usually have the health, taste, or social concerns we just described. Since they're not planning to give up meat entirely, none of those issues are really relevant to them.

The main barrier they confront is convenience: they, too, think vegetarian food is hard to find and difficult to prepare (Lea *et al.* 2006).

PUT YOURSELF IN THEIR (LEATHER) SHOES

One study found that for every person who had changed their eating habits to protect animals or the environment, five more intended to change but hadn't (Latvala *et al.*). What gives? Why do so many people have the same beliefs as vegetarians, but haven't put those ethics into action?

It's easy to discount people's reasons for not making a switch. Vegetarians dealt with all of the same issues omnivores did, and we were able to give up meat! It's tempting to tell ourselves there must be something wrong with meat-eaters: they're either stupid, lazy, or unethical, or maybe all three. While our instinct is to jump to such judgments, we need to put ourselves in other people's shoes.

Imagine that a friend of yours sat you down and told you about how terrible sweatshops are. Most likely you'd nod your head in agreement—what a shame they treat people that way! But what if your friend wanted you to stop buying anything from sweatshops? She had already done so, and now she wanted you to do the same. Would you make the change?

Probably not. It's too difficult, we'd tell ourselves. A lot of the things we buy are made in sweatshops. We'd have to start reading labels and looking into every brand— that's too much work! We'd have to give up our smart phone. We might have to give up our favorite clothing line. We couldn't buy cool toys for our nieces and nephews around the holidays. And even if we made all these sacrifices, the sweatshops would still be open. People would still be suffering. So, why bother? We already do a lot of good things for the world. This is one we'll just have to forget about.

Many meat-eaters feel the same way. They don't like how animals are treated, but giving up meat seems too difficult. We may think it's easy to be vegetarian, but to them it seems daunting. They see major barriers that we no longer notice.

To help more people make the switch, vegetarian advocates need to knock down those barriers. We need to do everything we can to provide simple, practical tips on how to find and make vegetarian food. We need to let people know it's okay to start slow if they're concerned about their health or giving up the foods they love. We need to make sure people realize the health benefits of ditching meat, and we need to show them how to be healthy as vegetarians. We also need to introduce people to tasty meat-free meals.

If advocates of vegetarian eating do all these things, a few years down the line many more people will be shaking their heads at meat-eaters and saying, "What do you mean you can't go vegetarian? It's so easy!"

9

FORMER VEGETARIANS

NO ONE LIKES A QUITTER

IF YOU'RE VEGETARIAN, YOU'VE DEFINITELY HEARD THESE six dreaded words come up in conversation: "I used to be a vegetarian. . . ." It can be frustrating to those who have given up meat to hear former vegetarians talk about why they've put animals back on their plates.

Just who are these ex-vegetarians anyway? How many of them are there? Why did they go back to eating meat? What separates them from those of us who've remained faithful to tofu? And how can we stop the flow of people returning to meat's bloody arms?

HOW MANY ARE THERE?

How many vegetarians go back to eating meat? We don't know for sure. The best estimate is that at least three-quarters of self-proclaimed vegetarians eventually return to meat.

The studies done so far have found recidivism rates of around 40–63 percent in the U.K., 60 percent in Canada, and 75 percent in the U.S. (Ruby 2012; The Modern Canadian Male; Survey for National Vegetarian Week; Herzog 2011) Unfortunately, these numbers aren't very precise. Most come from surveying the public to see how many current and former vegetarians there are. If a study found twice as many former vegetarians as current ones, it would suggest that about two-thirds of vegetarians go back to eating meat. But that's not really true.

For one thing, you could only find out if a person really stayed vegetarian by surveying them on their deathbed! The studies above included vegetarians of all ages, many of whom may ditch meat later in life. For another thing, rates of recidivism may be different for each generation. Vegetarian eating is much easier now than it was ten or twenty years ago, so fewer people might go back to consuming meat. On the other hand, the fact that vegetarianism is more popular now could mean more people are jumping on and off the bandwagon.

Lastly, most of these surveys relied on people's self-definition of whether or not they were vegetarian. As we saw earlier, most "vegetarians" still eat meat. So, it's a pretty safe assumption that most former "vegetarians" ate meat as well. We have no idea how the recidivism rate of real vegetarians compares to that of self-proclaimed vegetarians.

The bottom line is that we don't really know how many vegetarians go back to eating meat. What we do know is that for every person walking around proclaiming he or she's a vegetarian, there are two to three other people saying they used to be. It's probably realistic to estimate that at least three out of every four self-proclaimed vegetarians will eventually go back to eating meat.

Wow! What a staggeringly high number! If eating vegetarian is so good for your health, for animals, and for the environment, what does it mean when 75 percent of those people who try it can't stick with it?

It means people are facing (or feel they're facing) some serious hurdles in trying to stay meat-free.

WHY THEY'RE QUITTING

Former vegetarians point to four main reasons for going back to meat. Of course, these are self-reported—no one is going to say they stopped being vegetarian because they were too lazy to stick with it. For some, these reasons might be little more than justifications. Still, it's clear that people confront some persistent issues in trying to stay vegetarian.

In study after study, health concerns were the main reason people went back to eating meat. Most of these centered on fatigue and anemia, although some people worried they weren't getting enough protein. Vegans sometimes worried about calcium or vitamin B_{12} deficiencies (Ruby 2012; Herzog 2011; Haverstock and Forgays 2012; Barr and Chapman 2002).

One small-scale study discovered that nearly half of *current* vegetarians experienced temporary health issues after they ditched meat. Anemia was the most common problem; nearly a quarter of those in the study had been diagnosed as anemic

(Boyle 2011). It's interesting—and sad—that so many new vegetarians have health problems. The majority of people who stuck with a vegetarian diet said they ultimately felt healthier as a result of the switch (Do You Consider Yourself).

The health issues new vegetarians face aren't related to their reasons for ditching meat. People who go vegetarian to protect animals and those who go vegetarian to improve their health seem equally likely to go back to eating meat as a result of health problems. In one study, 57 percent of backsliders had initially gone vegetarian to protect animals. Just 15 percent had switched for their health, and another 15 percent had changed to protect the environment. Even among this animal-oriented group, health concerns were the number-one reason people returned to eating meat (Herzog 2011).

So in addition to touting the health benefits of cutting out or cutting back on meat, we need to show people *how* to be healthy as vegetarians. Giving them information on where they can get iron and protein is what's most important. Vitamin B_{12} and calcium deficiency may also be concerns for those who are going vegan. If we don't arm people with basic knowledge on how to be healthy as vegetarians, many more will return to eating meat.

But health concerns aren't the only thing driving people away from a cruelty-free diet. Taste is another factor. Some former vegetarians craved meat and were bored with the food they were eating. Others thought it was too inconvenient to be vegetarian. For them, vegetarian food was difficult and time-consuming to prepare, and it was hard to find it in restaurants and grocery stores. Lastly, some ex-vegetarians considered it difficult to eat with their omnivorous friends, or they began living with people who ate meat (Ruby 2012; Herzog 2011; Haverstock and Forgays 2012; Barr and Chapman 2002).

One study found that direct social support—whether from family, friends, online networks, or vegetarian-related groups—was important for helping people to stay vegetarian. Having easy access to good food also increased people's chances of sticking with a cruelty-free diet (Maintaining Vegetarian Diets).

Of course, most of us who stayed vegetarian ran into the same problems that former vegetarians did. We simply had the commitment to work through them. So it's tempting to look at former vegetarians with a sneer and think, "If I can do it, they can too." But that attitude certainly isn't going to help animals. Instead, we should look to these studies for insight into how we can help more people remain meat-free.

THE POWER OF HOW

The biggest lesson for vegetarian advocates is this: In addition to telling people why they should go vegetarian, we need to show people how to do it. Vegetarian advocates focus so much on the *whys* of going vegetarian that we often neglect the *hows*. But knowing how to do something is just as important as knowing why. A meta-analysis of hundreds of studies found that people's sense of self-efficacy—their feeling that they were able to change a behavior—was the best predictor of whether or not they actually would. Their self-efficacy was an even better predictor than their beliefs about how important it was to change (Sheeran 2006). The point is that people who don't know how to ditch meat won't ditch meat—even if they really want to.

Nearly everyone who goes back to eating meat has a *how*-related reason for doing so. They didn't know how to eat healthfully. They didn't know how to find and cook vegetarian food. They didn't know how to satisfy their cravings for meat, or how to eat out with non-vegetarian friends.

Only one study revealed former vegetarians who had gone back to meat because they no longer believed the ethical *whys* of vegetarianism; and even in that study it was a paltry 3 percent of ex-vegetarians (Herzog 2011). The study didn't share what these reasons were. Maybe they no longer felt it was wrong to kill animals. Maybe they had started buying free-range meat, or stopped believing that being a vegetarian really helped the environment. Whatever the reason, they made up only a tiny sliver of former vegetarians.

The bottom line is that people aren't going back to meat because they think it's the right thing to do. They're doing so because they're having practical difficulties with being vegetarian. While vegetarian advocates can't beat ourselves up for every person that stops being a vegetarian, we can redouble our efforts to provide helpful information on the key *how* areas of meat-free eating: health, taste, convenience, and social issues.

FORMER VEGETARIANS: THEY'RE JUST DIFFERENT FROM YOU AND ME

Aside from the fact that former vegetarians are eating meat again, are there any ways they differ from current vegetarians? Understanding those differences might help vegetarian advocates do a better job of keeping people from returning to meat.

As we saw earlier, the reason someone goes vegetarian doesn't seem to have a big impact on whether they stay meat-free. One study found that current vegetarians care a lot more about animal welfare, and only slightly more about their health, than former vegetarians (Haverstock and Forgays 2012). This could mean that caring about animals is important for sticking with a cruelty-free diet. On the other hand, former vegetarians might just say they care less about animals to avoid having their values contradict their diet.

A *Vegetarian Times* survey found health and ethical vegetarians were about equally likely to stay vegetarian over a three-year period. Environmental vegetarians were most likely to stick with a meat-free diet, but because there were so few of them to measure we have no idea how they really compare to health or ethical vegetarians (Stahler, Retention Survey).

The bottom line is this: While it's possible that people who care about the ethical issues of eating meat are more likely to stay vegetarian than those motivated purely by health concerns, the difference doesn't seem too large.

Moving on, one study showed that the way people went vegetarian mattered. Former vegetarians were more likely than current vegetarians to have stopped eating meat all at once. Those who stayed vegetarian were more likely to have switched gradually. Maybe that's because a gradual change is easier, both for the person going vegetarian and also for their friends and family (Haverstock and Forgays 2012). The takeaway for vegetarian advocates? They should encourage people to take the first steps toward meat-free eating, not encourage them to go from omnivore to vegan in one meal.

Self-identity might also play a role. One study indicated that current vegetarians said their food choices were an important part of who they are. Former vegetarians claimed this was never the case for them, even when they first ditched meat.

Why might identity play a role in whether people stay vegetarian? It's a fact of human psychology that we don't like to change our sense of self. So the more we see being vegetarian as part of our identity, the harder it is to go back to meat (Haverstock and Forgays 2012).

Does joining vegetarian groups help people stay meat-free? It might. One study discovered that those who stayed vegetarian were more likely to have joined a vegetarian potluck group, message board, or other social circle (Haverstock and Forgays 2012). In another study, vegetarians said having social support helped them stick with their diet (Maintaining Vegetarian Diets). On the other hand, the *Vegetarian Times* survey found that people were equally likely to stay vegetarian over a three-year period whether or not they belonged to a vegetarian or animal rights group, and whether or not they subscribed to a vegetarian magazine (Stahler, Retention Survey).

WHICH GROUPS ARE MOST LIKELY TO BACKSLIDE?

The *Vegetarian Times* study also found a few demographic differences between those who stayed vegetarian and those who went back to eating meat.

Age was one of the biggest differences. Although young people are more likely to go vegetarian, they are also more likely to quit being vegetarian. Of those in their twenties, 21 percent had gone back to eating meat over the course of the three-year study. For every older age group, 7 percent or fewer had gone back to meat (Chlebowski). (Teenagers weren't included in the study.) These results match the results of another study, in which the average age at which people went back to eating meat was twenty-five years old (Barr and Chapman 2002).

How long someone had been vegetarian also mattered a lot. Among those who had been vegetarian for less than a year when the study started, only 67 percent were still vegetarian three years later. Among those who had been vegetarian one or two years when the study started, 78 percent stayed vegetarian. For all other groups—those who had been vegetarian three years or more when the study began—93 percent to 100 percent stayed vegetarian.

So the *Vegetarian Times* study suggests that those in their twenties and those who have been vegetarian for fewer than three years are the people most likely to go back to eating meat. We have no idea how teenagers compare since they weren't included in the study.

Two final demographic notes are worth sharing. First, gender didn't matter. Men and women in this study were equally likely to stay vegetarian. Second, vegans and vegetarians had the same likelihood of going back to meat. By the time the three-year study was over, 6 percent of each group had resumed eating meat. Meanwhile, another 8 percent of vegans had gone back to being vegetarian. And 11 percent of vegetarians had moved up to vegan status (Chlebowski).

WHAT THEY EAT NOW

With so many vegetarians going back to eating meat, are there any silver linings to be glimpsed? Thankfully, there are two.

The first is that, although they're eating meat again, former vegetarians are at least eating less meat than the general public. A study of Canadian women found ex-vegetarians were more likely to have eaten some plant-based protein sources that week, such as beans, tofu, nuts, and lentils. Although they were no longer vegetarians, these women still replaced a portion of their meat with animal-friendly alternatives (Barr and Chapman 2002).

A broader U.S. study confirmed the trend. Of those vegetarians who had returned to eating meat, only a third said that they were now regular meat-eaters. Half were just occasional meat-eaters. One out of ten said they were now pescatarian, and another 10 percent said they only ate meat when there wasn't a vegetarian option available. No differences existed between the eating habits of male and female former vegetarians (Haverstock and Forgays 2012).

A person's initial motivation for going vegetarian might influence how much meat they eat once they've fallen off the wagon. One survey found that those who had initially ditched meat for ethical reasons ate less of it after backsliding than those who had initially stopped being vegetarian for social reasons (Herzog 2011).

HOW LONG WERE THEY VEGETARIAN?

The second silver lining is that most vegetarians don't go back to consuming meat right away. They often rack up a number of years of cruelty-free eating first.

One study suggested that ex-vegetarians had been meat-free for an average of nine years before returning to omnivorism (Herzog 2011). Another study showed they'd been vegetarian for three and a half years (Barr and Chapman 2002). A third study found they'd been vegetarian for at least five years before going back to meat. In that study, only 20 percent had lasted a year or less as vegetarians, 20 percent lasted one to two years, 30 percent lasted three to five years, 10 percent lasted six to ten years, and 20 percent lasted ten years or more (Haverstock and Forgays 2012).

Looking at these studies as a group, we can estimate that former vegetarians lasted about five years on average before going back to meat.

Is that good? Well, by comparison, it's a lot better than people who diet to lose weight! One study found that while two-thirds of those who went vegetarian or semi-vegetarian lasted at least a year, two-thirds of those dieting to lose weight called it quits in the first three months. The median length of time a person ate vegetarian or semi-vegetarian was two years. For those dieting to lose weight, it was just three months (Smith *et al.* 2000).

This information might leave vegetarian advocates a little dejected. After all, more than three-quarters of the people they persuade to go vegetarian will eventually start eating meat again! Well, they can cheer up, because there's one final bit of good news. It comes from calculating the answer to this question: How many years of vegetarian eating do we get for each member of the public who's persuaded to go meat-free?

Assuming they're persuading people twenty-five and under to make the switch, vegetarian advocates get the equivalent of about fifteen to twenty years worth of vegetarian eating for each person they convince to stop eating meat. And that's even after accounting for all of the backsliders! There are two reasons the number is so high. First, people who do stay vegetarian will live about fifty years. And second, many of those who go back to eating meat will still consume less meat than the average after they go back to their old ways.

So cheer up, vegetarian advocates! Even with all of the recidivism, for every person you persuade to ditch meat hundreds of farm animals will be spared a lifetime of misery.

DOCTORS DITCHING VEGETARIANISM

While it means very little in the grand scheme of things, here's one last groan-inducing finding about ex-vegetarians.

One survey tracked two thousand students at fifteen American medical schools from the time they entered school until the time they graduated. The study showed that rates of vegetarianism actually dropped over time. As freshmen, 8 percent reported being vegetarian. By the time they graduated, only 6 percent were (Beardsworth and Bryman 2004). The drop in vegetarianism was mirrored by a sharp fall in the percentage of students who thought nutrition counseling and healthful eating were important.

The study suggests that, whether intentionally or unintentionally, medical schools are leading the next generation of doctors to think eating healthily is not important. And that may be causing a number of medical-school students—those who were vegetarian for health reasons—to go back to eating meat. Unfortunate though those numbers may be, they may reflect accurately the nature of the medical establishment we currently have in the United States.

Thankfully, we don't need a doctor's note to tell us that staying vegetarian is the right thing to do.

10

RISE OF THE MEAT TOOTH

MEAT CONSUMPTION AT HOME
AND AROUND THE GLOBE

A NATION OF MEAT LOVERS

Although things are starting to change, America is still a nation obsessed with meat. Remember, this is the country that invented the KFC Double Down (a bacon-and-cheese sandwich in which the bun is replaced by two chicken patties) and the Wing Bowl (a televised chicken-wing-eating competition, with 2012's winner scarfing down an ungodly 337 wings).

Perhaps it should come as no surprise then that the United States inhales more meat per person than almost every other country on Earth. As of 2007, only tiny Luxembourg out-chomped the U.S. in per capita meat consumption. That year, Americans ate almost 50 percent more meat than Britons, four times more meat than Egyptians, and nearly twenty times more than the average Indian (Kings of the Carnivores; Statistics). With those sorts of numbers, it's easy to see why America also ranks as the world's most obese nation (Obesity). We're number one! We're number one!

Just how much do Americans love their meat? Agricultural economists Lusk and Norwood used price-elasticity data to find out. (Price elasticity refers to the fact that people will buy more or less of something based on how much it costs.) Lusk and Norwood discovered that people value meat more than any other food they eat at home. In other words, even when the price of meat goes up, people buy almost as much of it as they did before. Meat is more important to them than fruits, vegetables, cereals, non-alcoholic beverages, and other products. Meat is four times more important to them than dairy, and sixteen times more than sweets and sugars (Lusk and Norwood 2009).

Far from a sweet tooth, what Americans really have is a meat tooth. They will wreck their arteries, kill animals, trash the planet, and shell out a lot of money (if necessary)—all in the name of getting their next meat fix.

THE CENTURY OF MEAT

The twentieth century was without a doubt the most wretched period in history for farm animals. It saw the rise of intensive confinement systems as the main method of animal husbandry throughout the industrialized world. As a result, farm animals suffer much more today than they did one hundred years ago. Factory-farming practices are now spreading into rapidly industrializing countries, such as China, India, and Mexico—meaning the twenty-first century could be an even more miserable one for animals.

What's more, factory farming's ruthless efficiency has lowered the price of animal products. As a result of decreasing prices and increasing incomes, America's per capita meat consumption has risen by about 50 percent over the past hundred years. The European Union and other industrialized parts of the world also have seen a steep increase in the amount of meat eaten, although Americans have consistently ingested more animal flesh per person than their European counterparts (Download).

The rise in meat consumption has been even steeper around the planet: global per capita meat consumption has nearly doubled in the past fifty years (Kings of the Carnivores). Aside from a handful of African nations where meat consumption has stayed the same or declined slightly due to poverty, nearly all countries are eating more meat per person today than they were half a century ago (Speedy 2003). Developing countries are driving much of the increase. Today, people in the global South eat 25 percent more meat than they did just fifteen years ago. Per capita consumption in developed countries rose only 2 percent during that time (Nierenberg and Reynolds).

Once you factor in human population growth, the picture for animals becomes even grimmer. Fifty years ago, 70 million tons of meat was eaten around the world (Kings of the Carnivores). Today, that number stands at 300 million tons—a fourfold increase (Nierenberg and Reynolds). About half of that increase is because the world now has over seven billion people, as opposed to three billion in 1960; about half is due to increases in per capita consumption.

Most devastating of all for animals is the fact that much of the increased meat-eating, both in the U.S. and abroad, is because of a rise in the consumption of chickens. While individual Americans are eating only slightly more red meat and fish today than they were in the early 1900s, they're eating *seven* times as much chicken (USDA, Poultry Slaughter). Globally, per capita poultry consumption rates are about five times higher than they were just fifty years ago. While poultry represented just 12 percent of all meat eaten around the world in 1963, it's now up to 31 percent (Kings of the Carnivores). Chicken is expected to pass pork in the next few years to become the world's most popular meat (Nierenberg and Reynolds).

As a result of the growth in population and the sharp increase in per capita chicken consumption, billions more animals are suffering on U.S. farms today than did in the mid-1900s. In 1945, U.S. farms raised only 366 million broilers. Today, that number tops seven billion (Broiler; Report: Number of Animals).

Ironically, billions *more* chickens would experience the horrors of factory farms if the poultry industry hadn't succeeded in nearly doubling the average live weight of broiler hens at slaughter, and dramatically reducing mortality rates on the farm (USDA, U.S. Broiler Industry). Although the reduced mortality is good for the total number of animals, since it means fewer of them suffer to death, the increased weight has serious downsides to the welfare of those who are born and die, as we discussed earlier.

What this means is that around the globe as you read this, tens of billions more chickens are suffering than did half a century ago—a result of both human population growth and a rise in the amount of chicken being eaten per person. What's more, the proportion of hens being raised in intensive factory-farm conditions has been growing, and will continue to do so over the next few decades.

A NEW HOPE

Before you start weeping at the horror of it all, we should remember the good news— at least in the U.S. As of 2012, per capita meat consumption and demand have been dropping steadily since hitting a high point in 2006. This fall was the first sustained lowering in average consumption since the Great Depression (Horowitz).

Between 2006 and 2012, per capita beef consumption sank from 66 to 57 pounds. Pork consumption fell from 49 to 45 pounds. Turkey consumption went from 17 to 16 pounds. And, most importantly of all, chicken consumption dropped from 86 to

80 pounds. All told, Americans were eating close to 10 percent less meat in 2012 compared to just six years earlier. As a result, hundreds of millions of farm animals were spared a lifetime of misery in 2012.

Wait, you may say. *It's great that consumption has been going down, but what's actually causing this?* Higher prices may be one reason. In recent years, corn prices have gone up significantly, thanks in large part to the grain's use in ethanol production. Because corn is commonly used as feed for farm animals, higher prices mean more expensive meat. Other meat production costs may also have risen due to drought, increased fuel prices, and other factors. As we've learned, higher meat prices mean people will buy slightly less meat.

Or maybe the major recession that hit in late 2007 is to blame for the drop in meat consumption. Or how about the big uptick in unemployment? These are all good questions. And thankfully we have answers, courtesy of Dr. Sethu and his analysis of USDA data at CountingAnimals.com.

Rising costs were indeed part of the reason that Americans were eating less meat. But there was also decreased demand for each type of meat between 2006 and 2012. In other words, Americans *wanted* to eat less meat. In fact, nearly 70 percent of the decline in beef consumption and over 90 percent of the decline in eating chicken seems to have been caused by lower demand for these products.

How do we know? If rising costs were the only thing making Americans eat less meat, then we should have seen a 4.1 percent drop in beef consumption and a 0.4 percent drop in chicken consumption. These percentages are based on the price elasticity of each product—in other words, how purchasing is usually affected when prices go up or down. What we actually saw was a 13.6 percent drop in beef consumption and a 6.6 percent drop in chicken consumption. Therefore, the main reason Americans were taking meat off of their plates was because they didn't want it there.

And what about the downturn in the economy? A recent meta-analysis of hundreds of studies found that, in industrialized countries, people who experience a drop in income actually eat more meat. When individual incomes go down, people tend to eat more chicken and pork, and roughly the same amount of beef and fish (Sethu, Meat Consumption; Gallet 2010). So the economic downtown and the higher rates of unemployment probably didn't lead Americans to eat less meat. If anything, it should have led them to eat more.

This is all great news. Not only were Americans eating less meat as of 2012, they *wanted* to be eating less meat. As a result, hundreds of millions of farm animals were being spared a lifetime of misery each year.

NATURE VS. NURTURE

Just as the family we grow up in affects who we become, the political, financial, and geographic circumstances of a country affect how much meat it consumes.

Among countries whose citizens have a high average income, there is little country-to-country difference in how much meat each citizen eats. Say you put into a hat the names of the twenty-five countries with the highest average income levels. You then put your hand in the hat, fished around, and pulled out two: Denmark and France. Let's say you happened to know that the average French person makes about $4,500 more per year than the average Dane. Unfortunately, that information would be of no help to you in predicting which nation eats more meat.

One piece of data, however, does allow you to determine more accurately which high-income country consumes more meat. The piece of data? How equally wealth is distributed in each country. High-income countries with more equal distribution of wealth tend to eat less chicken and beef, with no increased consumption of other meat products (Morris).

Why would this be the case? The researchers who discovered this intriguing finding speculate that countries with a more egalitarian society are also more compassionate toward animals. Countries that haven't yet extended that spirit of concern throughout human society have also failed to extend it to farm animals. There's other evidence that countries with a more equal distribution of wealth care more about farm animals: they tend to regulate factory farming more strictly (Morris).

As we take a broader look around the world, and leaving aside wealth distribution among individual citizens, we can see one factor that really predicts how much meat any particular country eats: Gross Domestic Product (GDP). (GDP is the value of all goods and services produced by a country each year.) Per capita GDP is strongly related to meat consumption. Along with population growth, growth of GDP has led to dramatically higher rates of meat consumption around the globe.

In Asia, each $1,000 increase in per capita GDP corresponds to a 3-pound rise in meat consumption. In Africa, the same GDP growth leads to a 4-pound growth. In the global North it corresponds to an average 6-pound increase, and in the Middle East higher GDP leads to a whopping 9-pound rise.

While East Asians don't increase their red- and white-meat consumption as much as other regions as their GDP increases, their fish consumption goes up much more. A $1,000 increase in per capita GDP leads Asian nations to consume 5 pounds more fish per capita, compared to about 2 pounds in Western, African, and Middle Eastern nations.

A few other national and geographic factors influence how much meat people eat. For one thing, countries with more of their population living in urban areas eat more red and white meat. This phenomenon might be attributable to the fact that such populations have access to a wider variety of food, or are more likely to have access to refrigeration. Or it could simply be that urbanization goes hand-in-hand with an increase in GDP, and we know that as GDP increases so meat consumption rises. Fish consumption doesn't seem to be impacted by how urban a country's population is.

Climate also matters. Nations in temperate climates consume a whopping 42 pounds more meat per year than those in arctic and subarctic regions. They also eat 24 pounds more meat per year than those in tropical regions. Part of the reason for this discrepancy might be that temperate climates are better for growing grain, which can be fed to farm animals. GDP could also play a role, since most high-GDP countries are in temperate zones. Climate does not seem to have an impact on fish consumption.

Nations with more land per capita also eat more meat. This makes sense, since animal agriculture requires a lot of acreage for pasture and growing feed crops. Lastly, nations with more water area (oceans, seas, lakes, etc.) per capita consume more fish. No surprise there.

BACK HOME IN THE USA: HOW MUCH MEAT IS ON AMERICAN PLATES?

We have already found out that Americans eat more meat per capita than almost any other people on the planet. But among Americans, who are the true kings of carnivorism? Which gender, age, income, education, and ethnic groups eat the greatest number of farm animals?

That sounds like a grim question, but it's actually a very useful one for vegetarian advocates to answer. If we want to spare as many farm animals as possible, then targeting those groups that eat the most animals could be helpful. Of course, we also have to consider how likely each group is to change (a subject covered earlier).

To find out just how much meat Americans eat, we turn to the comprehensive National Health and Nutrition Examination Survey (NHANES). NHANES is undertaken regularly by the U.S. government to track Americans' eating habits over time. Data are collected by asking people to list everything they've eaten in the past twenty-four hours. Researchers then break down what people ate into specific food groups. For example, they determine approximately how many pounds of chicken are in an average serving of chicken casserole (USDA ERS, Commodity Consumption).

The NHANES data we'll cite below was collected between 1999 and 2004. It's possible that things have changed since then, but this information is the most recent released.

In calculating how many animals each group kills per year, we translated the NHANES data into current consumption rates. In other words, a group that ate a perfectly average amount of meat, dairy products, and eggs in 1999–2004 is considered to be killing 33 farm animals today. That is the number of animals today's average meat-eater kills.

Without further ado, let's find out which groups put the most—and fewest— animals on their plates!

AGE

People in their twenties and thirties eat far more meat than any other age group. Consumption of pork, beef, turkey, and chicken peaks among those who are aged twenty to forty, then slopes downward among older people. The only two products that have a later peak are fish and eggs. People in their forties and fifties eat the most fish and eggs.

One other unique aspect of age is that teenagers eat very little fish: twelve to nineteen year olds eat well under half the amount of fish that every other age group eats. On the other hand, teenagers eat only slightly less beef, chicken, pork, and turkey than average (USDA ERS, Commodity Consumption; Stahler, How Many Youth).

For other demographic groups, we're going to calculate how many farm animals each group kills. For example, we're going to take a look at whether the rich kill more or fewer animals than those with lower incomes. But it doesn't make sense to do this for age groups. Why? Because, employing the logic we discovered earlier in this book, it's irrational to expend effort in vegetarian advocacy on the age group that kills the most animals.

Although a person usually has the same gender, education level, and ethnicity throughout the course of their life, their age will change. If you convince someone to go vegetarian when they're a teenager, you'll curb their impact on animals before they even reach the peak meat-eating years of their twenties and thirties. In general, the earlier in life you persuade someone to go vegetarian the less meat they will eat over the course of their life.

The bottom line is we don't need to worry about exactly how many animals each age group kills.

GENDER

When it comes to meat consumption, men and women were not created equal. While American women ate around 155 pounds of meat per year at the turn of this century, men scarfed down nearly 240 pounds—or 50 percent more per person than women. Men ate more meat in every major category. They ate about 27 percent more fish, 29 percent more chicken, 48 percent more turkey, 65 percent more pork, and 79 percent more beef. When you break these numbers down to the per-animal level, men are responsible for the death of 37 farm animals each year. Women kill only 29 farm animals. Put in percentage form, men butcher about 28 percent more farm animals than women.

These facts hold true across all ethnicities (USDA, Commodity Consumption). The only exception is Asian women, who eat even less meat compared to Asian men than you would expect based on gender differences (Gossard and York 2003).

The bottom line? If men and women were equally likely to respond to vegetarian advocacy, and were equally responsible for food-purchasing decisions, men would be the better group for vegetarian advocates to target. After all, getting just four men to go vegetarian should help slightly more farm animals than getting five women to make the switch.

As we saw earlier though, women are a much better target audience. They are twice as likely to go vegetarian or to cut back on meat, and they control more household food-purchasing decisions. They also seem to be a lot more likely than men to be persuaded by vegetarian outreach.

INCOME

When we separate people based on their age or gender, we see clear differences in the amount of meat each group eats. When we divide Americans based on how much they earn, things don't break down so cleanly.

Overall, people who make more money eat more meat. As we move up the economic ladder, consumption rises from 189 pounds (low income) to 195 pounds (middle income) to 204 pounds a year (high income). Low income in the NHANES data is defined as less than 185 percent of the poverty line. Middle income is 185–300 percent of the poverty line, and high income is over 300 percent of the poverty line.

Although total meat consumption rises in line with income, the number of animals killed does not. That's because different groups eat different types of meat. Low- and high-income groups eat more chicken than those in the middle class. High-income earners also eat more fish and more eggs (USDA ERS, Commodity Consumption).

So which group hurts the greatest number of farm animals? In a year, those with low incomes kill about 32 farm animals; middle-income earners are responsible for the deaths of about 30; and those with high incomes take the lives of about 34.

While those with high incomes kill more farm animals than others, the difference is not nearly as dramatic as it is between people of different genders or ethnicities. Targeting vegetarian advocacy toward groups with certain income levels would make only a modest difference in the number of animals spared.

Here's one last interesting point about income and meat consumption. As we've seen, those with high incomes eat more meat than those in the low-income group. But as we also saw earlier, people do not eat more meat when their individual income goes up. In fact, the data suggest that as one person's income goes up, their meat consumption actually goes down (Gallet 2010). So the general class that a person belongs to, and the changes in that person's income over time, seem to have competing influences on how much meat they eat.

EDUCATION

The NHANES data found that as educational level increases, meat consumption does as well. This is true of overall meat consumption, and it's also true of poultry and fish consumption.

Does that mean that education inspires people to eat more meat? Not necessarily. Educational level is closely related to income. The more you learn, the more you earn. As we just saw, the more you earn the more meat you eat. So it's possible that people with more education eat more meat simply because they have higher incomes (US EPA).

The most recent data indicate that people who do not complete high school kill about 29 farm animals each year. High school graduates end the lives of about 34 farm animals each year. And those who continue their education past high school butcher an average of 35 farm animals per year. As of 2004, those in the top educational bracket killed about 20 percent more farm animals than those in the lowest.

The situation may be changing though. Between 1988 and 2004, overall meat consumption (as well as poultry and seafood consumption specifically) rose most rapidly among those with less than a high school education. It appears that people with lower education levels are starting to catch up to their more educated peers when it comes to how many animals they eat (Wang *et al.* 2010).

ETHNICITY

Major differences exist between ethnic groups when it comes to meat consumption. African-Americans eat dramatically more of every category of meat except beef. Compared to Caucasians, African-Americans eat 70 percent more fish, 55 percent more chicken, 39 percent more turkey, and 10 percent more pork. These numbers are even more striking when you consider that African-Americans have in general lower income and education levels than Caucasians—factors that should have led to lower meat consumption (Ryan and Siebens 2012).

All told, African-Americans consume an average of 236 pounds of meat per year. Caucasians, Hispanics, and other ethnic groups (when you combine all remaining ethnic groups into one category) each consume between 191 and 193 pounds per year.

African-Americans kill a mammoth 46 farm animals each year. Caucasians cause the deaths of 31 farm animals; Hispanics, 33; and other ethnicities—when combined into one group—also dispatch about 33 farm animals each year. So while Caucasians, Hispanics, and "others" slaughter about the same number of farm animals, African-Americans kill almost 40 percent more (USDA ERS, Commodity Consumption).

This situation may be changing a bit. Data from 2004 suggest the overall gap between African-Americans and other ethnicities had begun to narrow a little. However, the discrepancy between African-American women and women of other ethnicities had actually widened by 2004 (USDA ERS, Commodity Consumption; Wang *et al.* 2010).

The bottom line? Inspiring African-Americans to go vegetarian or cut back on meat should spare many more animals than getting Caucasians or Hispanics to do the same. Depending on how receptive they are to advocacy efforts, African-Americans might be a great group for vegetarian advocates to target.

CHECKING IN ON CHICKEN: A FEW NOTES ABOUT POULTRY CONSUMPTION

As we've discussed at length, nearly all of the farm animals people eat are chickens. So there's really one main factor that determines which demographic groups kill the most: chicken consumption. Nearly all of the difference between groups is due to how much chicken they eat.

Let's say we combined all other animals—cows for beef and dairy, turkeys, pigs, farm-raised fish, and egg-industry hens—into one group, and called it "all other farm animals." If we compared the demographic groups, we'd see that there's never more than a two-animal difference between groups when it comes to killing "all other farm animals." Every demographic group kills between four and six of these "all other farm animals."

The reason men slaughter a lot more farm animals than women, and African-Americans kill a lot more than other ethnicities, is because they eat more chicken. It's true that men and African-Americans eat more of other animal products as well. But in terms of the number of farm animals killed, those other products basically don't matter. This reality highlights again just how important an issue chicken consumption is for vegetarian advocates. Because it's so important, let's take a few minutes to learn a little more about how and why Americans eat poultry.

Although men eat many more pounds of chicken than women do, women choose chicken slightly more often. The difference is not large, however. As of 2004, 34 percent of the meat women ate was chicken, compared to 30 percent for men.

We know that chicken consumption in the U.S rose significantly through 2006. Were both men and women piling up the chicken, or was one gender more responsible for that increase? It looks like, as of 1999–2004, men and women were increasing their chicken consumption at about an even rate.

What demographic groups are eating the most chicken? We saw earlier that African-Americans eat a lot more chicken than other ethnic groups. We also saw that those in their twenties and thirties, and those with higher education levels, eat more chicken.

When it comes to income, we saw that those with low and high incomes eat more chicken than those in the middle class. A 2002 National Chicken Council survey found similar results. It discovered that the most frequent chicken consumers were those with incomes of over $95,000 a year in 2012 dollars. It also found that people in their thirties and forties, and those in the south and northeast regions of the U.S., ate chicken more frequently (Consumers Rate Chicken).

What do consumers think about chicken? As we know, many people perceive the flesh to be healthier than red meat. But they see other differences as well.

A 1990s study from the U.K. found that, compared to eating beef, eating chicken was seen by consumers as more likely to cause cruelty to animals, more likely to exploit poorer nations, and more likely to result in food poisoning (Heller). Another study discovered that while warnings about the cholesterol and fat content of meat did not lead people to eat less chicken, warnings about meat safety did (Davidow). If advocates of vegetarian eating want to steer the public away from consuming chicken, they may want to talk about issues like animal cruelty and food safety, since those are concerns people already have about chicken.

What do people like about chicken? The U.K. study revealed that chicken was seen as less likely to increase cholesterol levels and less likely to contain hormones, antibiotics, or additives. It was perceived as more convenient and having more value per dollar than beef (Heller). A U.S. chicken-industry study carried out in 2002 found that the main aspects people liked about chicken were its versatility and convenience, the fact that it is healthier and lower in fat than red meat, is cheaper, and that the meat is more tender. Eighteen- to twenty-four-year-olds cited convenience, health, and flavor as their main reasons for choosing chicken (Consumers Rate Chicken). A 2011 survey of Dutch consumers found that one reason women chose chicken was to avoid the sight of blood or bones that might be noticed in other types of meat (de Boer and Aiking 2011).

GIVING UP RED MEAT: A GOOD OR BAD THING?

The biggest problem that farm animals in the U.S. have faced over the past fifty years is not the rise in population. It's not even that Americans are eating a lot more meat per person now than they were half a century ago. The biggest problem is the dramatically increased demand for chicken.

Between 1975 and 2005, beef consumption dropped by 23 pounds per person. Pork and fish consumption stayed about the same. Poultry consumption, on the other hand, increased by a jaw-dropping 57 pounds per year. Out of these pounds, 49 were from people eating more chicken, and 8 were from people eating more turkey (Sethu, Meat Consumption). As a result of the increase in chicken consumption, the number of farm animals killed in the U.S. each year has skyrocketed.

There are two stories going on over the past half-century. The first is that Americans have been eating more and more meat, and virtually all of that new meat has been poultry. The second is that Americans have been cutting back on beef and replacing it with chicken. Until 2006, there seemed to be a clear inverse relationship between chicken and beef consumption. As one went up, the other went down. Incredibly, that inverse relationship seems to have been broken. From 2006 to 2012, per capita consumption of both beef and chicken (as well as turkey and pork) steadily decreased. Consumer demand for each of these products also went down (Sethu, Meat Consumption). Although beef saw the largest drop in consumption, the declines in every category were significant. As of 2012, at the national level a drop in beef consumption now appears to have gone hand in hand with a drop in chicken consumption.

As you can probably guess, this is great news for farm animals! People weren't just replacing beef with chicken, a decision which would have led many more animals to suffer. They were taking meat off their plates entirely.

Those are the general trends in America through the end of 2012. But how do those trends relate to individual consumers?

Over the past few decades, a growing number of people have sworn off red meat for good—often for health reasons, though studies show that a number of people who give up red meat do so for animal welfare or environmental reasons, or because they are disgusted by it (Santos and Booth 1996; de Boer and Aiking 2011). As a result, there are a lot of red-meat avoiders around. National polls have found that about 6 percent of Americans say they never eat red meat (Stahler, How Many Adults; How

Many Vegetarians, 2003). A very thorough British study, which asked respondents to report everything they'd eaten over seven days, found that about 5 percent of Britons ate little to no red meat (Aston *et al.* 2012).

Most vegetarians see this as a good thing. *Oh that's great*, they think. *They're not all the way to vegetarian, but at least they got rid of red meat!* A lot of people see those who have given up red meat as being halfway between omnivore and vegetarian.

Although giving up red meat is a healthy thing to do, does it also have a positive impact for animals? The answer hinges on this question: Do people who give up red meat eat more chicken than they used to? If they do—even a small amount more—than their decision to stop eating red meat actually has negative consequences for animals, at least in the short term. More animals will suffer and die. In fact, even if red-meat avoiders replaced 95 percent of their red meat with tofu, and just 5 percent of it with extra chicken, the results would still be bad for animals. They would be sparing a fraction of a pig and a fraction of a cow from suffering, but causing an additional two birds to suffer.

If red-meat avoiders were to replace all of their red meat with chicken, the results would be disastrous. Whereas the average meat-eater kills 33 farm animals a year, these red-meat avoiders would kill 69 farm animals a year. By cutting out red meat and replacing it with chicken, they would be harming twice as many farm animals. It is sad and ironic that people who cut out red meat because they care about animals could end up hurting more animals than the average omnivore.

Clearly, this is a frightening proposition. But is that what really happens?

People who *reduce* the amount of red meat they eat by a slight to moderate amount do tend to eat more chicken. A comprehensive study of meat consumption in Britain, carried out by the British government and using seven-day dietary recollections to measure what food people ate, divided respondents into five tiers based on how much red meat they ate. People in the low tier—Britons who ate the least red meat—consumed about 60 percent more chicken than those who ate the most red meat. So if there's anything vegetarian advocates can do to prevent people from replacing red meat with chicken, they should do it.

Men in the lowest tier also ate up to 60 percent more fish, although fewer eggs, than men who ate the most red meat. Fish and egg consumption did not vary much in women. (Aston *et al.* 2012).

The picture changes, though, when we look at those who have cut out red meat entirely or almost entirely. When we look at these red-meat avoiders overall, they do not seem to have a negative impact on animals.

There are only two known studies that found people who stop eating red meat but continue eating other meat products end up eating more chicken. Both are studies of teenagers in the 1990s.

One 1997 study of Australian teens found that women who avoided red meat did eat more chicken meals than omnivores. The study did not measure exactly how much additional chicken was eaten (Worsley and Skrzypiec 1997). A very small 1996 Canadian study of fifteen red-meat avoiders had teenagers spend three days weighing and recording all of the food that they ate. Although the researchers do not directly state that red-meat avoiders ate more chicken than omnivores, we can extrapolate that they did from their data. Among this small group of teenagers, red-meat avoiders appear to have eaten roughly 30 percent more chicken (and fish) than omnivores (Donovan and Gibson 1996; Per Capita Poultry Consumption; Calories in Food).

There's one important thing to note about these two studies. Most of the red-meat avoiders in the studies were not motivated by health concerns. Concern for animals seemed to be their most common reason for ditching red meat, followed by a dislike of its taste. Health concerns came in third (Worsley and Skrzypiec 1997; Donovan and Gibson 1996). Among the general population, motivations for cutting out red meat come in the reverse order.

Aside from those two teenager-specific studies, there isn't any evidence that people who give up red meat end up eating more chicken. Other surveys on the subject have found no difference in chicken-consumption rates between people who eat red meat and people who don't, but do eat chicken.

A 1998 study of 350 London-area residents found that people who reported eating a standard diet and people who reported eating a diet low in red meat consumed roughly the same amount of poultry (Pollard *et al.* 1998).

The comprehensive British National Diet and Health Survey noted, "At the individual level, the intake of white meat was not correlated with that of either red or processed meat." In other words, at the individual level, people who ate less red meat did not eat more poultry than the rest of the population (Aston *et al.* 2012).

Some studies found that red-meat avoiders actually ate less chicken than omnivores. A 2001 Australian study reported that meat-eaters who ate little to no red meat consumed chicken slightly less often than those who ate red meat (Lea, Moving From

Meat). A 2011 survey of female college students in the U.S. found that those who had given up red meat but not other animal products ate chicken significantly less often than omnivores. Omnivores reported eating chicken 4.5 times a week, whereas red-meat avoiders reported eating chicken only 2.7 times per week (Forestell *et al.* 2012).

When we look at all of these studies in total, it appears that people who cut red meat out of their diet do not end up eating more animals. They may not have much of a positive impact for animals. But on average, they don't seem to have a negative effect. It's possible that teenagers are one group that might replace red meat with chicken, especially teenagers motivated by animal welfare concerns. When vegetarian advocates are encouraging teenagers to cut out meat, they may want to put extra emphasis on why cutting out chicken is the best place to start.

One more thing to consider when judging whether red-meat avoiders are good or bad for animals is whether, for a number of people, cutting out red meat leads them later to cut out all meat. A 2011 Dutch study found that those who cut out red meat have a relatively negative perception of meat in general (de Boer and Aiking 2011). Cutting out red meat can be—and for some people is—a stepping-stone to full vegetarianism. We don't know what percentage of red-meat avoiders go on to take the next step. But a number of them do, and that has to be factored in when considering their ultimate impact on animals.

FISH TALES

Right now, Americans eat only a modest number of farm-raised fish. A conservative estimate puts the figure at a little more than one farm-raised fish per person per year. Still, aside from chickens, Americans eat more farm-raised fish than any other farm animal.

As we discussed earlier, fish on fish farms lead terrible lives. Animal welfare expert Dr. Sara Shields rated them as one of the most abused farm animals. Farm-raised fish also live very long lives, meaning they experience prolonged suffering (Farm Animal Welfare). What's more, many dozens of small wild fish are caught and killed as food for each farm-raised fish.

Among people who do cut out meat, fish is usually the last to go. One study showed that even self-described vegetarians ate fish an average of about once a week (Forestell *et al.* 2012). Another study found that a full quarter of British college students who considered themselves vegetarians and who did not eat chicken continued to eat fish (Santos and Booth 1996).

The good news is that fish consumption in the U.S. has stayed about the same over the past hundred years. Americans eat far less fish than they do beef or pork. So, why isn't fish more popular?

The main reason people choose fish is for its flavor, though some people also turn to it for health reasons. On the other hand, many consumers say that the smell and sometimes the taste of fish are big reasons for not eating it more often. People also say they have trouble cooking fish themselves, in part because of the bones. Convenience and price are also factors. Prepared fish meals aren't as readily available as chicken, beef, or pork options, and fish can be pricey. Teenagers, who eat fish much less often than adults, cite the smell of fish as the biggest turn-off (Verbeke and Vackier 2005).

What can advocates of vegetarian eating take away from these studies? In addition to talking about the cruelty fish endure, advocates may also want to mention the health risks of eating fish, and emphasize the bad smell and bones that can characterize fish meals. Messages like these should help inspire more people to leave fish off their plate.

11

MEAT 2.0

WHAT VEGETARIANS AND MEAT-EATERS
REALLY THINK OF VEGETARIAN MEATS

VEGETARIAN MEAT IS A BIG DEAL. THERE WOULD BE FAR
fewer vegetarians in the industrialized world if vegetarian burgers, patties, hot dogs,
chicken nuggets, and similar products didn't exist. Whether made of soy, wheat, or—
in the case of the popular European product Quorn™—fungus, these products have
one thing in common: their meaty texture, flavor, and aroma can satisfy even the most
carnivorous cravings.

But just how popular are vegetarian meats? Who eats them? What types of vegetarian meats do omnivores prefer? And if you're going to prepare a vegetarian meal
for meat-eating friends, what does the research suggest you do to get them to love it?

VEGETARIAN MEAT'S STORIED ROOTS

In the U.S., the quality of vegetarian meats has increased dramatically over the past
two decades. Talk to anyone who's been vegetarian since the early 1990s, and they'll
tell you horror stories of the cardboard-tasting products they used to buy from the
health-food store. It's the vegetarian equivalent of, *When I was a kid, I used to have to
walk three miles to school in the snow with no shoes.* Their point is that new vegetarians
don't know how good they have it. Even mainstream grocery stores now stock whole
shelves of mouth-watering plant-based meats, which seem to taste better with each
passing year.

Vegetarian meats may be more popular now than ever before, but if you thought
they were a new phenomenon, think again. They've been bought and sold in the U.S.
as far back as the late nineteenth century, when you could order them through the
mail from the Battle Creek Sanitarium in Michigan, a health and wellness center

run by the Seventh Day Adventist Church. In addition to creating the first vegetarian meats, the Sanitarium also popularized the use of nuts and nut butters as meat replacements. In a sales pitch that might not work so well today, they promoted nuts as being "nearly equivalent in blood-making qualities to a pound and a quarter of beefsteak."

The unlikely duo that created the first line of plant-based meats was John Harvey Kellogg—the man behind Kellogg's breakfast cereals—and an Assistant Secretary of the USDA, Dr. Charles Dabney. Kellogg and Dabney wanted to develop a product that had the taste and texture of meat, but which was healthier and cheaper so that poor Americans could enjoy it.

Two of their early products were Nuttose, a mixture of ground-up nuts and cereal grains, and Granose, a wheat-based biscuit meant to mimic a fillet of beef. But their breakout success was Protose, a mixture of wheat gluten, grains, and ground peanuts that resembled beef or mutton. As spokesperson (and Civil War hero and Red Cross founder) Clara Barton declared, "Protose looks like meat, tastes like meat, contains the same nutritive properties, and is an absolutely pure product of the animal kingdom." Labeled as "vegetable meat," and sold at a lower price than canned meat, Protose was promoted as a substitute for breakfast meats, steaks, and even picnic sandwiches. By 1912, 144,000 pounds of Protose were being sold annually across the U.S. Its sales run lasted over a hundred years until Morningstar Foods, the inheritors of Protose, pulled it from their product line in 2000.

Vegetarian meat had its fans from the beginning. In the early 1900s, major newspapers praised it as almost indistinguishable from the real thing. The *Chicago Tribune* regularly printed recipes for meat-replacement dishes. Vegetarian chicken croquettes and fish cakes were served at gala events to politicians who didn't realize they were eating faux meat. The Vegetarian Meat Company, a competitor to Battle Creek, opened its doors in Washington, D.C., in 1910 (Shprintzen 2012).

A hundred years later, U.S. retail sales of soy-based meats have topped $630 million and have been rising steadily for years. Overall sales of vegan specialty products passed $2 billion in 2009 (Priority Ventures Group). Walmart and Target stock vegan chicken patties, baseball stadiums offer vegetarian hot dogs, and mainstream newspapers gush over the meat-like consistency of new products like Beyond Meat™. In the U.K., sales of meat-free and "free-from" foods reached £950 million in 2012 (Statistics). Perhaps the deluge of new meat substitutes is why only a quarter of British vegetarians are unhappy with the vegetarian offerings at their supermarket (Public Attitudes/Consumer Behavior).

John Harvey Kellogg's work in the late 1800s has had lasting effects on the meat-free foods we eat, from our cereal-laden breakfast table to our lunchtime peanut butter sandwiches to our dinner plates piled high with savory vegetarian meats.

WHO EATS VEGETARIAN MEATS?

Just who is chowing down on today's meatless meats?

A lot of people: 15 percent of Dutch consumers and 20 percent of U.K. residents say they eat vegetarian meats at least once a week. Less frequent users make up another 16 percent of the Netherlands' population and another 35 percent of Brits. A 2005 U.S. study discovered that 6 percent of Americans frequently purchased and 17 percent occasionally purchased vegetarian meats (Hoek *et al.*, Replacement of Meat). Still, there's a long way to go. A United Soybean Board survey found that only half of all American consumers were familiar with veggie burgers and tofu, and fewer still knew about vegetarian hot dogs and other soy-based meats (Priority Ventures Group).

Vegetarians aren't the only ones tucking into mock meats. One study indicated that among those who ate vegetarian meats at least once a week, two-thirds were meat-eaters (Hoek *et al.*, Replacement of Meat). A 1999 study found that 80 percent of mock-meat consumers were not vegetarian (Chapman). Vegetarians do love their mock meats though. Half of British vegetarians eat them at least weekly, and in the Netherlands that figure is an enormous 85 percent (Hoek *et al.*, Replacement of Meat).

Demographically, vegetarian-meat consumers (whether vegetarian or omnivore) look a lot like vegetarians. They tend to be better educated, have higher incomes, be younger, live in smaller households, and live in more urban areas. Overall, women are more likely than men to eat plant-based meats. But when you look at carnivores who eat mock meat, or are occasional consumers of plant-based meats, the gender gap is not large (Schosler *et al.* 2012; Hoek *et al.*, Replacement of Meat; de Boer and Aiking 2011). One study found that Hispanic households were twice as likely as white households to report eating vegetarian meats, with African-Americans scoring highest on a few meat-free items (Heller).

WHY PEOPLE EAT (OR DON'T EAT)
VEGETARIAN MEATS

Why do some meat-eaters choose Tofurky® over turkey when filling up their shopping cart?

In terms of their attitudes and motivations, omnivorous mock meat–eaters stand at a halfway point between vegetarians and regular omnivores. They don't hold strong food ideologies, but they have some uneasiness with how meat is produced. They are interested in eating less meat, have a lower appreciation for meat, and are more interested in going vegetarian (Hoek *et al.* 2004; de Boer and Aiking 2011). This is particularly true among heavy users of vegetarian meats, many of whom are motivated by a concern for animals. Light users are more often solely interested in trying out new foods (Hoek *et al.*, Replacement of Meat). For all groups, the desire to eat healthfully is another motivating factor.

Not surprisingly, the more people eat vegetarian meats the more they like them. Heavy users think vegetarian meats are healthier, more convenient, better tasting, more luxurious, and more ethical than meat. Light to medium users feel the same way, but not as strongly. However, even heavy users of vegetarian meats find animal meats more familiar and satisfying (Hoek *et al.*, Replacement of Meat; Hoek 2010).

A Dutch study found that one out of every ten meat-eaters said they preferred the taste of plant-based meats to animal meats (de Boer and Aiking 2011). That's impressive when you consider that two-thirds of the Dutch have never tried or only rarely eaten vegetarian meats (Hoek *et al.*, Replacement of Meat). In several blind taste tests, consumers actually preferred meat-free burgers and partially meat-free pizza toppings to the original meat versions (Roche; Qammar *et al.* 2010).

Why don't more meat-eaters pick up vegetarian meats? A pair of studies found the main barriers were practical concerns. People said that buying vegetarian meats was inconvenient and that they didn't know how to prepare them (Bosman *et al.* 2009; Gunert 2006). But there are two other big concerns omnivores have: vegetarian meats are unfamiliar, and may not look, smell, or taste appetizing to them (Hoek *et al.*, Replacement of Meat).

In other words, some meat-eaters are scared. Ground-up bloody entrails of an animal? Easy to prepare and delicious to eat! Ground up seasoned mixture of beans and plants? Disgusting! Joking aside, the fact is that most people are averse to trying new foods. The closer vegetarian meats come to the real thing, the more willing meat-eaters will be to eat them.

Interestingly though, it's not just taste, familiarity, and convenience that matter. People's beliefs about the world seem to influence their food choices, including what they think of vegetarian meat.

In a 2008 Australian study, researchers discovered a vegetarian sausage that meat-eaters couldn't tell from the real thing. In trying to pick out which sausage was meat and which was vegetarian, two-thirds of them guessed wrong. Researchers then presented the sausages to a new group of study participants. Some participants were told that the vegetarian sausage was vegetarian and that the meat sausage was meat. Others were lied to about which was which. People sampled each sausage, and rated how it tasted.

Overall, the sausages were rated as being equally tasty. But something interesting happened when you divided respondents up based on their beliefs about the world. Prior to the taste test, each person had filled out a survey that measured whether they thought having social power was very important or whether they were more egalitarian. Those who valued social power said the sausage labeled as real meat tasted better. This was true both when the sausage was actually meat, and when—unbeknownst to them—it was actually vegetarian sausage that had been falsely labeled. Respondents who were more egalitarian thought the sausage labeled vegetarian tasted better— even when, unbeknownst to them, they were actually eating the meat one (Allen *et al.* 2008).

So it wasn't just the taste and smell of the sausage that influenced how delicious people perceived it to be. People were also influenced by what the food symbolized to them. If it fit in with their values, it tasted better. If not, it tasted worse.

Getting the public to buy and enjoy vegetarian meats, then, is not just a question of creating a product that tastes identical to meat. It's also a matter of getting the values people attach to vegetarian meats to be values embraced by most Americans. Eating vegetarian chicken strips needs to become as American as eating apple pie.

Unfortunately, the deck may be stacked against animals when it comes to how people value food. One study revealed that people rate different foods as having different levels of status. Fish and red meat came first, then poultry, followed by dairy, fruits, and vegetables. Cereals—the predominant foodstuff of many vegetarians—came dead last. Sorry vegetarians, but your food is just not prestigious!

The study discovered that people are more likely to prefer foods higher up the food-status ladder. People who are self-conscious about what others think of them are particularly likely to seek high-status foods (Allen 2005).

LAYING IT ON THE TABLE: WHICH MEAT SUBSTITUTES ARE LIKED BEST?

Some vegetarians turn up their noses at plant-based meats, calling them overly processed, unhealthful, and expensive. But many vegetarians and meat reducers depend on them for keeping their meals cruelty-free. Of all the protein-rich plant products out there, vegetarian meats seem to be the most popular among those who are starting to cut out meat.

One Dutch study asked meat reducers which products they usually replaced meat with. Respondents were able to pick out up to three products from a list. Unfortunately, the top choices were all animal products: 76 percent answered fish (which is meat, of course), followed by eggs at 49 percent, and then cheese at 34 percent. Among potentially vegan fare, mock meats topped the list at 26 percent. They led lentils and beans (17 percent), tofu (14 percent), nuts (9 percent), tempeh (3 percent) and seitan (1 percent) in popularity as a meat replacer (Schosler et al. 2012).

Another study by the same researchers found similar results: familiar dishes were most popular, followed by mock-meat dishes, with tofu dishes coming in last. In this study, meat-eaters were given pictures and descriptions of different meals and asked to rank them from best to worst. Their rankings went as follows: omelet, pasta with pesto, minced mock meat in tomato sauce, couscous with chickpeas and vegetables, stir fry with seitan, mock-meat steak, stir fry with tofu and vegetables, a tofu snack, and an Indian lentil dish. It should be noted that this was a Dutch study; Americans might have answered differently (Schosler et al. 2012).

For people who choose meat alternatives, how do they pick one over the other? One study showed that taste is key when choosing a vegetarian meat, followed by price, fat content, and convenience (Maurer). The less often a person eats vegetarian meat, the more important it is to them that it closely resemble the real thing. Taste and texture seem to be more significant than appearance or smell in judging how similar a product is to animal meat (Hoek et al., Replacement of Meat).

In one study, vegetarian versions of processed meats were seen as being the most similar to real meat. Vegetarian sausages were ranked highest, with vegetarian burgers, balls, breaded meats, and minced meat also seen as somewhat similar to the real thing. Plant-based versions of unprocessed chicken, pork, and beef weren't seen as very similar to the original (Hoek *et al.,* Identification of New Food Alternatives). As a result, we might conclude that vegetarian processed-meat products go over best with the general public. In fact, a 2008 industry report in the U.K. found it was pieces (such as chicken or beef nuggets), meat snacks (like jerky), and mince that were driving the growth of the vegetarian-meat market (Consumers Prefer Meat-Free).

Because it's more similar to meat, vegetarian meat is more preferred by most people than tofu. Studies show that vegetarian meat usually ranks higher when it comes to texture, flavor, aroma, overall comparability with meat, and intention to use (Schosler *et al.* 2012; McIlveen *et al.* 1999; Elzerman *et al.* 2011; Hoek 2010).

Similarity to meat becomes less important once a meat substitute is part of a meal. The flavors and textures of the meal seem to mask many of the individual differences between products (Elzerman *et al.* 2011). One study on chicken, Quorn™, and tofu found that, although meat-eaters rated each product differently, they were equally happy with their overall meal (Hoek 2010).

So perhaps just as important as the meat substitute itself is the meal it comes in. The meal narrows the difference between meat and meat substitutes, as well as between individual vegetarian products. It can make or break how much people like vegetarian meat, and whether they continue eating it.

Thankfully, some good research from the field of food science can help us make meat-free meals as tasty as possible when we're cooking for friends and family. This research shows that when other elements of the meal are familiar, people enjoy the meal more and are more willing to try unfamiliar foods. Adding familiar seasonings and sauces will help a mock-meat dish go over well (Elzerman *et al.* 2011). And don't skimp on those side dishes! Having familiar and tasty side dishes is also helpful when the main dish is an unfamiliar one (Wansink 2002).

Most American families are used to the traditional three-part meal of meat, vegetables, and starch. So when preparing meat-free meals, it may be better to keep the same format and simply substitute a plant-based meat for an animal-based one. It's probably also better to introduce vegetarian meats gradually. It will help people see them as something interesting and new, and give people time to get used to them (Schosler *et al.* 2012; Wansink 2002).

If you want to make sure your guests aren't hungry again two hours after eating, protein is essential. High-protein vegetarian meats have been shown not only to fill people up more than low-protein vegetarian meats do, but to do so more than animal meats (Hoek 2010; Stubbs *et al.* 2000).

One final, important aspect to keep in mind when it comes to which vegetarian meats are best is to think about which do the most good for animals. It's a plus when someone replaces beef or pork with vegetarian meat. But it's a hundred times better for animals when someone substitutes vegetarian meat for chicken. Whether they swap their chicken sandwich for a vegetarian-chicken sandwich or with a vegetarian burger doesn't matter. But since many people may want to replace their meat with a similar product, it's particularly important for advocates of vegetarian eating to promote great vegetarian-chicken products.

Unfortunately, some vegetarian meats could be worse for animals than the flesh they replace. Many frozen vegetarian meats contain egg. A veggie burger with egg in it probably caused more suffering and killed more animals than the beef burger it was meant to replace. When promoting vegetarian meats, animal advocates should make sure the items are free of all animal products.

LANGUAGE MATTERS, PART 1: VEGETARIAN, VEGAN, OR MEAT-FREE?

When encouraging people to switch to vegetarian meats, the words advocates use can make a difference. Some phrases appeal to meat-eaters and others may turn them off.

A study by British trade magazine *The Grocer* found the public was more likely to embrace vegetarian meats when the products were labeled "meat-free" than when they were labeled "vegetarian" (Consumers Prefer Meat Free). Over the past five years an increasing number of British supermarkets and vegetarian-meat producers have switched from "vegetarian" to "meat-free," and they are seeing increased sales among meat-eaters (Jamieson).

Vegetarian-meat companies in the U.S. are doing the same. Pick up a bag of Gardein™ chicken, and you'll see the label "I'm meat-free!" Tofurky® hot dogs boast a label of "meatless." Lightlife labels their products "meat-free," or notes that they are packed with "veggie protein." Almost none of their products still carries a prominent "vegetarian" label.

Why does "meat-free" seem to go over better than "vegetarian" with the general public? Industry experts think the term "vegetarian" has negative connotations. Perhaps, due to guilt, social norms, or other reasons, people simply look down on all things "vegetarian." The word might also conjure up memories of a flavorless tofu burger they tried once.

Unfortunately, people's expectations about whether they will like a dish have a major impact on whether or not they do. If they expect it to taste bad, it will. For example, in one study people were given a nutrition bar and asked to rate how it tasted. Although the bars were identical, some had a label saying they contained soy and others didn't. None of the bars actually had any soy in them. But the bars that supposedly had soy were rated as tasting much worse than those that didn't. People expect soy products to taste bad, and that expectation led them to think the nutrition bar tasted worse (Wansink *et al.* 2000). Other taste-test studies have found similar results (Cooney 2011).

The point is this: when you label something in a way that makes people expect something to taste bad, it probably will. For whatever reason, many people think that "vegetarian" products will not taste good. They don't seem to have as negative a perception about products labeled "meat-free." So when sharing your tasty vegan chicken salad with co-workers, you'll probably get a better response by calling it "meat-free" than by calling it "vegan" or "vegetarian."

The same may apply when promoting cruelty-free eating. Encouraging people to go meat-free, or to ditch meat, may be more persuasive than encouraging people to go vegetarian. Since people seem to expect "meat-free" food to taste better than "vegetarian" food, switching to "meat-free" food should seem easier.

Using the word "vegetarian" also raises the sticky issue of self-identity. As we saw earlier, the public may think of vegetarians as a distinct group of people who are different from normal (!) Americans. That's not good. We don't want people to think they need to take on a new identity to cut cruelty out of their diet. Why? Because most people are loath to change their sense of who they are.

For example, if you were a Democrat, which of these statements would sound more palatable to you: "You should become a Republican," or "You should vote Republican"? The first statement focuses on your identity, while the second focuses on your behavior. The second statement is probably more palatable to most Democrats. Similarly, "eating meat-free foods" or "not eating meat" may be more palatable to most omnivores than "going vegetarian."

All that being said, "meat-free" might not go over well at all with certain audiences or in certain contexts. A study carried out by Mercy For Animals and the Humane Research Council found that young women aged thirteen to thirty-five reported they liked the term "vegetarian" much more than "meat-free." They also liked it more than "vegan" or "meatless." A full 36 percent of respondents said that if they saw an online advertisement for a free vegetarian brochure, they would be extremely likely or very likely to click on it. Only 14–16 percent said the same for a "free meat-free brochure" or a "free meatless brochure," and 21 percent for a "free vegan brochure." Perhaps young women view the term "vegetarian" much more favorably than other groups. Or perhaps context matters—so that while "meat-free" is useful on product labels it is less effective when promoting dietary change among certain groups (Humane Research Council, Results from MFA Survey).

LANGUAGE MATTERS, PART II: GOOD LABELS AND BAD LABELS

When it comes to getting people to enjoy meat-free food, mentioning that it has soy in it is a bad idea.

We said earlier that people considered a nutrition bar less tasty when the label noted it contained soy. Among taste-conscious consumers, the bar that was not labeled as having soy was rated better in nearly every category measured, including texture, healthiness, appearance, feeling good about eating it, and being likely to purchase it. Even health-conscious consumers said they were less likely to buy the one with soy in it (Wansink *et al.* 2000).

Other tests have found the same thing: soy labels make regular customers enjoy the food less, and they have at best a neutral impact on vegetarians and health-conscious shoppers. Even researchers funded by the National Soy Board advise food companies not to tout the presence of soy in their products (Wansink 2003; Wansink and Park 2002).

So we know not to use the "soy" label. How about calling food "healthy"? Does a "healthy" label lead people to like food more, less, or the same? The data are mixed. In some studies, for some products, and with some audiences, the "healthy" label led people to like a product more. But in many situations, it led people to like it less. In other studies, the label had no impact (Wansink *et al.* 2004; Horgen and Brownell 2002; Wansink *et al.* 2000).

Are there any labels that would lead people to like meatless meals more?

An appetizing descriptive phrase should do the trick. By describing the food in mouth-watering terms, we set positive expectations about how the food will taste. Since people tend to taste what they expect to taste, these descriptions will lead people to enjoy the food more (Mela 1999; Kahkonen and Tuorila 1998).

One study found that the use of descriptive labels in a restaurant led people to like the food more and to want to dine at the restaurant again. A similar study was conducted and similar results found in a cafeteria setting. Menu items that were given descriptive phrases had increased sales and were rated as more tasty, flavorful, and satisfying (Wansink *et al.* 2001).

So rather than bringing "healthy vegan soy-chicken salad" to the family barbeque, try bringing "zesty meat-free chicken salad with fresh parsley and onion." Because Romeo was wrong: a rose by any other name is not just as sweet. If we want to change habits and save lives, we need to satisfy the taste buds. The words we use can make a big difference in how effective we are at doing that.

12

ANIMALS ARE STUPID, EMOTIONLESS, AND DON'T FEEL PAIN

HOW EATING MEAT AFFECTS
BELIEFS ABOUT ANIMALS

THERE ARE PLENTY OF REASONS FOR WHY PEOPLE EAT MEAT. Their families and friends do it, they were raised doing it, they like the taste of it, it's the most convenient way to eat, and so on.

But one small part of the equation is this: eating meat leads people to view farm animals differently. Ask a meat-eater and a vegetarian how intelligent, how emotionally complex, and how sentient a pig is (how much it can feel pleasure and pain), and chances are you'll get different answers. Especially if you ask around lunchtime.

MORAL DISENGAGEMENT

To start, let's talk about "moral disengagement." One way that we humans avoid feeling guilty when we hurt others, or lessen our sadness when we hear about tragedies going on in the world, is by subconsciously thinking less of those who suffer. *They are not like us*, we tell ourselves. *Therefore, what's going on is okay … or at least not as bad as if it were happening to me or my family.*

During wartime, the enemy is always presented as different from and less human than us. This is moral disengagement in action. In order to fend off pangs of guilt or sadness, we denigrate those that suffer. For example, researchers studying the phenomenon have found that we ascribe fewer secondary emotions—regret, nostalgia, and melancholy—to those we have hurt (Castano and Giner-Sorolla 2006). It makes sense for our brains to want to do that. The more base and stupid the other person is, the less reason we have to feel bad. What better way to soothe our troubled conscience so we can carry on with life as usual?

Not surprisingly, the same phenomenon holds true when it comes to the animals people eat. Meat-eaters don't want to think that they're harming intelligent, emotionally complex, and sentient individuals. But rather than go vegetarian, most people choose to reassure themselves that animals are stupid, emotionally simple, and unable to feel pain.

PAYING NO MIND TO ANIMALS

Meat-eaters and vegetarians are in general agreement that animals have primary emotions—such as fear, panic, happiness, and excitement. But vegetarians think that animals also have secondary emotions, such as guilt, nostalgia, and melancholy. Meat-eaters disagree. They believe these emotions are uniquely human and set people apart from the rest of the animal kingdom (Bilewicz *et al.* 2011). Depressed cat? No way. Guilt-ridden dog? Stop imaging things!

The gap between how vegetarians and meat-eaters see animals' minds gets even wider when it comes to those we eat. For example, vegetarians think that pigs and dogs have about the same emotional complexity. Meat-eaters don't think so. They see pigs as having a much more barren emotional life than dogs (Bilewicz *et al.* 2011).

The gap becomes a chasm when you connect an animal with the meat on a person's plate. In one study, meat-eaters were divided into two groups. One was told that they would be served meat at the end of the study. The other was told they'd be served fruit. Both groups were then asked their thoughts as to how much mental capacity farm animals had. The people who knew they were going to be eating meat thought farm animals had less mental capacity (Bastian *et al.* 2012). As soon as they heard they would be eating meat, the wheels of moral disengagement began to turn. That way, when the meat was served, they would feel less guilty about eating it.

In fact, simply connecting farm animals with meat triggers the same reaction. In another study, meat-eaters were divided into two groups. Each was given a picture of a lamb or cow and a short description. The first group was told: "This lamb/cow will be moved to other paddocks, and will spend most of its time eating grass with other lambs/cows." The second group was given the same pictures but a different description: "This lamb/cow will be taken to an abattoir, killed, butchered, and sent to supermarkets as meat products for humans." Participants in each group then rated how much mental capacity they believed that lamb or cow to have. People supplied with the second description—the one that reminded them the animal would be used for meat—rated the animal as having less mental capacity (Bastian *et al.* 2012).

Even thinking about the origins of meat is uncomfortable. To morally disengage, meat-eaters change their beliefs about how much mental capacity farm animals have.

THE QUESTION IS, CAN THEY SUFFER?

"The question is not, Can they reason? nor, Can they talk? but, Can they suffer?"

So said famed Utilitarian philosopher Jeremy Bentham in what would later become a rallying cry for the animal protection movement.

Compared to vegetarians, meat-eaters view animals—especially farm animals— as less intelligent and with fewer emotions. Do meat-eaters also think farm animals have less ability to suffer? It looks like they do. In fact, it appears that by merely classifying an animal as food, people consider that animal less able to suffer.

In one study, participants were given a paragraph about a fictional tree-dwelling kangaroo and its interactions with aboriginal people in Papua New Guinea. The descriptions in the text of what happened were varied. In some stories, the kangaroos were killed, and in others they weren't. In some descriptions, the kangaroos were killed by humans, and in others they died natural deaths. In some, the aboriginal people ate the kangaroos, and in others they didn't.

Participants read only one of the paragraphs and then ranked how much they thought the kangaroos were able to suffer. It turned out that simply having the kangaroos classified as human food led people to rate them as less able to suffer. That was true whether the kangaroos were hunted and killed by humans, or whether humans simply ate kangaroos that had died naturally by falling out of trees.

Simply calling an animal "food" led people to think that animal had less ability to suffer. What's more, that denial of the ability to experience pain led people also to care less about the animal. The less the kangaroos were perceived as being able to suffer, the less people cared about them (Bratanova *et al.* 2011).

In another study, researchers wanted to see what influenced people's concern for animals more: intelligence or sentience. In this study, participants were fed either beef or nuts and then asked how much moral concern they had for cows. They were also asked how intelligent and sentient they thought cows were. Those who had eaten meat had less moral concern for cows and rated them as less sentient (Loughnan *et al.* 2010).

Together, these studies show that denying animals' ability to suffer is another tool meat-eaters use to try to avoid the discomfort that comes with their food choices.

ANIMALS: ARE THEY LIKE US?

Beliefs about how sentient and intelligent animals are don't just impact people's decisions to eat or not eat meat. They also impact what types of animals people eat, and how comfortable they are with eating each one.

One study asked over three thousand students from across Europe and Asia to rank twelve animals in order of how sentient they were, with 12 meaning the animal was most able to feel, and 1 meaning it was least able to feel, relative to other animals.

Dogs and cats were ranked around 9. Pigs were ranked at about 6 and cows at about 5. Chickens came next at position number 4. Fish were ranked the lowest of all animals measured, with an average rank of 2. Interestingly, both vegetarians and non-vegetarians put animals in roughly the same order (Izmirli and Phillips 2011).

Studies that asked people to rate how intelligent animals are and how well they can communicate with humans have generated nearly identical rankings. Dogs and cats come first, followed at a distance by pigs and cows, then chickens and other birds, with fish at the bottom (Harrison 2010; Eddy *et al.* 1993).

Perhaps not surprisingly, these rankings of sentience and intelligence also align with how much empathy people have for animals. The less sentient and intelligent an animal appears to be, the less we care about it.

In one study, people were asked how much empathy they had for different animals on a one-to-ten scale (with 10 being the highest score). The study defined empathy as the belief that "I would be able to understand this animal/creature's feelings." Dogs and cats were rated in the 7 to 8 range, cows scored a 4, pigs were 3.5, and chickens 3. Goldfish, the only fish measured, scored a meager 1.

These varying levels of concern aren't just felt at the abstract, intellectual level. They also shape our immediate, subconscious response to different types of animals.

One team of researchers wanted to find out how people reacted to viewing animals in distressing situations. Specifically, they wanted to see whether those reactions differed based on the kind of animal that was in distress. The researchers created a series of short videos showing humans, primates, four-legged mammals, or birds being victimized. Each video included a close up of the face of the animal in pain, a scene of the animal being injured, a scene of the animal being confined, and a scene of the animal being hit or handled roughly.

Before participants in the study were shown each video, they were hooked up to two devices that would measure their physiological responses. The first was a skin-conductivity test, which would measure how much of an aroused emotional response they had to the video. The second was a corrugator EMG test, which would measure muscle activity in their face. It would track positive and negative emotional reactions to the video as they occurred.

So how did people respond to seeing each species in distress? After watching the videos, participants were asked to report how much concern they felt for each animal. On a 1–10 scale, they gave birds an average of 5 and four-legged mammals an average of 6. Primates and humans scored up in the 8–9 range.

When it came to how much empathy they felt for each animal, people weren't just talking the talk. Their bodies were walking the walk. The corrugator EMG and skin conductivity showed people had a slightly more empathic response to the video of four-legged mammals being hurt than they did to the video of birds being hurt. Their empathic responses to seeing humans and primates in distress were higher still. All in all, people's physiological reactions matched up well with their self-reported levels of distress, sympathy, and empathy for each species (Westbury and Neumann 2008).

The different levels of empathy we have for different species help explain why the public seems to feel less guilt about eating chicken and fish than they do about eating beef and pork. They also help explain why even ethical vegetarians usually give up red meat first, then chicken, with fish often being the last meat to go (if it ever does). Although chickens don't trail too far behind larger mammals in our empathy, intelligence, and sentience studies, fish have always ranked far down at the bottom.

Why do people consistently rank animals in this order? After all, most people know very little about how sentient and intelligent different species actually are.

Culture can certainly play a part. Dogs and cats rank higher because humans have chosen to keep them as pets, and as a result have come to know them much better than other species. But culture aside, the main basis for the rankings in this: the closer to us an animal is in evolutionary history, the smarter and more capable of feeling and communicating we perceive them to be. And the closer to us they are, the more we care about them (Harrison 2010; Eddy *et al.* 1993).

That's not just true for how we respond to other animals. It's true for how we respond to other people as well. Skin-conductivity tests have shown that African-Americans have more of an empathic response to pictures of other African-Americans suffering or having a good time than they do to pictures of Caucasians in the same circumstances. And Caucasians have more of a response to pictures of other Caucasians (Westbury and Neumann 2008). Studies have also demonstrated that we are more concerned about people related to us, even distantly so, than we are for the general public (Harrison 2010; Cialdini *et al.* 1997).

We seem to be hard-wired to care more about those who are similar to us, and to care less about those who aren't. Maybe this is genetic Darwinism at work: the more genetically similar another individual is to us, the more inclined we are to care about them. That similarity might also help us put ourselves in their shoes more easily.

Whatever the reason, humans do seem to have an innate tendency to care less for chickens and a lot less for fish, than they do for larger mammals. It's tragically unfortunate that the animals which are smallest—and therefore eaten in extremely large numbers—are also the animals people seem hard-wired to care least about.

ANIMALS AS PEOPLE

Unfortunately, moral disengagement works when it comes to eating animals. People decide on a subconscious level that farm animals are less intelligent, less emotionally complex, and in particular less able to feel physical and mental pain. These perceptual twists make it easier to continue eating meat without feeling guilty. The more mentally barren an animal is perceived to be, the more edible they become (Bastian *et al.* 2012).

Although it's unfortunate the human mind works this way, such knowledge can also tell animal advocates something about how to inspire more people to go vegetarian. Because the flipside of everything we've been discussing is this: the more sentient, emotionally complex, and intelligent people think an animal is, the less willing they are to eat it. The more similar the animal is to them, the more uncomfortable people are with causing it harm.

One study found that when people had first to consider the psychological attributes of an animal, their disgust at the idea of eating the creature increased and their interest in eating the animal declined (Ruby and Heine 2012). By emphasizing the emotional richness of farm animals, vegetarian advocates can be more effective at inspiring people to leave meat off their plates. This tactic includes the positive emotions of farm animals, like the loving concern they have for their children and the bonds of friendship they forge with one another. It also includes their mental anguish, such as the boredom and stress they feel being confined in a cage so small they can't turn around.

What is particularly effective is to describe an animal's mind, emotions, and personality in human ways. In one study, participants were told a story about a dog in jeopardy—for example one who was drowning in a lake. They were then asked if they would risk their life to try to save the dog. For half of the participants, the dog was depicted in bland terms: he had a good sense of smell, he was good with other dogs, and he listened to commands. For the other half, the dog was described in human-like terms: he had a good sense of humor, he got along well with others, he was a good listener. Those who had the dog described to them in the latter manner were significantly more likely to say they'd try to save the dog (Butterfield *et al.* 2012).

In a related study, people were shown pictures of dogs who were again portrayed in either neutral or human-like terms. The people who had dogs described in human-like terms were more willing to help the dog get adopted by volunteering at the animal shelter where the dog was being housed. They were also more likely to agree that eating meat and using animal products like leather were morally wrong (Butterfield *et al.* 2012).

So when encouraging people to stop eating meat, advocates of vegetarian eating shouldn't talk like a scientist. "Pigs have the emotional complexity to experience increased stress levels when subjected to intense confinement" is not compelling. A better way to phrase it would be, "Pigs trapped in gestation crates go crazy from the frustration and boredom of never being able to turn around."

Emphasizing the rich emotional experiences of animals, and their ability to suffer both physical and psychological pain, should make people less comfortable with eating meat. Describing these abilities and experiences in human-like terms that people can relate to should be particularly effective.

13

MEAT-FREE MEDIA

THE IMPACT OF BOOKS, VIDEOS, AND TELEVISION ON WHAT PEOPLE EAT

THE POWER OF BOOKS, MUSIC, VIDEOS, WEBSITES, AND other media to influence what we think and how we live our lives is undeniable. And that power includes the ability to inspire people to go vegetarian.

One study of vegetarians—conducted years before Facebook or YouTube even existed—found that nearly a third of them had changed their diet as a result of some form of media (MacNair 1998). A 2012 U.S. study indicated that number had risen to 43 percent (Haverstock and Forgays 2012). The rise of social media has made it easier than ever to come across pictures, videos, and information about the cruelty of animal agriculture and the benefits of vegetarian eating.

So just how big an impact can media have? A handful of studies document how media can succeed—or fail—at inspiring people to change their diet.

THE OMNIVORE'S DILEMMA

The Omnivore's Dilemma by food writer Michael Pollan and published in 2006 is not a pro-vegetarian book. In fact, Pollan sometimes aggravates vegetarians with his strident support for farming operations he perceives to be humane. But *Dilemma* is still an anti–factory farming book, and its descriptions of modern animal agriculture may be eye-opening to many readers. So just what impact does the book have on the eating habits of its readers?

Researcher Paul Rozin, who actually coined the phrase "the omnivore's dilemma," wanted to find out. In the fall of 2007, the entire freshman class at the University of Pennsylvania was required to read Pollan's book and discuss it as part of their orientation. Rozin surveyed students before, immediately following, and one year after reading the book to see what effect it had on their attitudes about food.

Compared to freshmen who hadn't read the book, students who had were more reluctant to eat meat, more interested in eating organic food, and more likely to think the quality of the U.S. food supply was declining. They were also more supportive of the environmental movement and more opposed to government corn subsidies. The more of the book they'd read, the more they felt that way.

A year later, however, several of those attitudes—including the reluctance to eat meat—had vanished. The only concerns that remained were on corn subsidies, food-supply quality, and the support for the environmental movement. On the other issues measured, students who had read *The Omnivore's Dilemma* actually cared *less*, and were now more comfortable with eating meat than those who hadn't read it.

The study didn't ask students why their attitudes had changed or whether their diets had shifted as a result of reading the book. It's possible that some students did start eating less meat. But in general, the book seems to have failed to make students less comfortable with factory farming or eating meat (Hormes *et al.*).

THE SIMPSONS

Lisa Simpson is probably the most famous cartoon vegetarian in the world. The influential television show *The Simpsons* has been running for over twenty-five years in the U.S., and Lisa's meat-free diet has been woven into the plotline of numerous episodes. It all started with Episode 133, "Lisa the Vegetarian," in which Lisa decides to go vegetarian after befriending a lamb at a petting zoo. Former Beatle Paul McCartney agreed to guest star in the episode under the condition that Lisa remain a vegetarian for the rest of the series.

One study looked at whether girls who watched Lisa go vegetarian would be inspired to do the same. In a laboratory setting, the episode was shown to nine- and ten-year-old girls who hadn't already seen it. They were then asked their thoughts on going vegetarian.

After watching the episode, the girls were more likely to believe something was wrong with eating meat. They were also about 10 percent more likely to intend to become a vegetarian, although that number dropped to 5 percent within a few weeks. The video also led the girls to believe it was more difficult to give up meat than they had previously thought. In the show, Lisa has a hard time going vegetarian—she's teased relentlessly by her family, friends, and neighbors for ditching meat (Byrd-Bredbenner *et al.* 2010).

Unfortunately, the study didn't track whether the girls actually changed their diets. But it did suggest that even a cartoon character can inspire people to want to ditch meat.

PAMPHLETS

Passing out booklets about factory farming and vegetarian eating is a common method vegetarian advocates use to encourage the public to ditch meat.

In 2012, The Humane League and Farm Sanctuary carried out a survey of 500 college students to see what impact getting a leaflet had on their diet. The surveys were filled out by a representative sample of students two to three months after they had gotten a leaflet. The study showed that about one out of every fifty students who received a booklet said they had gone vegetarian or pescatarian as a result. A quarter said they were eating less chicken and a third said they were eating less red meat. About a fifth said they were eating less fish, a fifth said they were eating less dairy, and a fifth said they were eating fewer eggs (Cooney, The Powerful Impact).

As we saw earlier, among the general public less than a quarter of those who say they're cutting back on meat are actually doing so. It's safe to assume that students are equally likely to say they changed when they didn't. Still, the study demonstrated just how powerful well-designed leaflets can be when targeted toward young people. Even after accounting for students over-reporting change, it appears that every two leaflets distributed on a college campus spares one farm animal per year from a life of misery.

ONLINE VIDEOS

Videos about the cruelty of factory farming may be one of the most effective ways of persuading people to cut out or cut back on meat.

A 2007 pork industry study polled children who had seen a YouTube video about factory farming or meat consumption. It found that one out of every three kids said the video had an impact on their meat consumption (Checkoff Tracks Activist Groups).

A 2012 study by the Humane Research Council found that, after seeing a powerful video about the cruelty of factory farming, 12 percent of viewers said they wanted to eliminate animal products from their diet. Another 36 percent said they were interested in cutting back. Videos on the environmental and health reasons to go vegetarian, as well as a video about a rescued farm animal, also led many viewers to want to cut out (7–10 percent) or cut back (27–31 percent) on animal products (VegFund Video Survey). Respondents in the survey were 500 randomly selected 15–23 year olds.

In 2011, The Humane League conducted follow-up surveys with teenagers who had seen a farm animal–cruelty video a few months earlier. They were only able to survey those who'd "liked" the video via Facebook, nearly a third of whom said they had eliminated chicken and red meat from their diet. Another third said they'd cut back on chicken and red meat. Half of the respondents said the video led them to cut out or cut back on fish, eggs, and dairy (The Humane League).

Both of these studies are probably also filled with over-reporting. Most people who said they cut back on meat, or intended to do so, probably didn't make a change. Still, the surveys are a testament to how powerful a tool online video is, especially when targeted toward young people. With millions of teenagers watching online videos about factory farming each year, it's no wonder the number of vegetarians, vegans, and meat reducers is climbing!

MEDIA COVERAGE OF FACTORY FARMING

How does the public respond to news stories about factory-farming investigations and legislation?

As we discussed earlier, in 2011 an undercover investigation into the slaughter of cattle exported from Australia to Indonesia received national news coverage across Australia. Two weeks after the story broke researchers surveyed the public to see what they thought of it. Some of those surveyed had seen coverage on TV, others on the Internet or in newspapers, and still others had heard the story on the radio.

The most common emotional response to the story was pity. Out of those who saw the coverage, 85 percent said they felt pity for the animals. Two-thirds felt sadness, anger toward those abusing the animals, and admiration for the investigators. Three-quarters were glad it was broadcast, though a fifth felt it was too graphic. Shockingly, 2 percent said they had sought counseling as a result of seeing the story.

Unfortunately, most people also felt that there was nothing they could do to help the situation. As a result, most of those over the age of thirty did nothing. Three percent said they donated to one of the animal protection charities that carried out the investigation, and 2 percent said they stopped eating meat or beef.

On the other hand, the coverage seemed to have had a larger impact on those under thirty. Among the 18–29 crowd, 16 percent said they stopped eating meat or beef and 11 percent said they donated to one of the animal protection charities involved. Across all age groups, women were more likely than men to respond positively to the investigation and to do something to try to help the situation (Tiplady *et al.* 2012).

In the United States, agricultural researchers at Kansas State and Purdue universities analyzed the impact media coverage can have on meat consumption. The study looked at how much coverage was given to animal welfare issues in the chicken, pork, and beef industries between 1999 and 2008 in major U.S. newspapers and magazines. It then compared that information with data on how consumer demand for meat rose and fell during those ten years. Most of the media coverage was about investigations of factory farms or farm animal–welfare legislation, or general stories on factory farming.

The researchers found that while demand for beef wasn't influenced by media coverage, demand for poultry and pork was. When stories about cruelty to chickens or pigs made headlines, the public ate fewer of those products. And they didn't just switch from one type of meat to another—they cut back on meat as a whole. The decreased demand for poultry and pork lasted up to six months after the news story broke.

The researchers estimate that over those ten years the demand for pork would have grown about 2.5 percent higher, and the demand for chicken 5 percent higher, if not for the media coverage (Tonsor and Olynk 2011). If they're right, it means that millions of pigs and hundreds of millions of chickens will be spared a lifetime of suffering each year as a result of ongoing media attention to farm animal welfare issues.

14

MESSAGES THAT MOTIVATE

SELLING THE BENEFITS OF A VEGETARIAN DIET

IN CHAPTER 7 WE LOOKED AT WHAT MOTIVATES PEOPLE TO cut out or cut back on meat. But just what do those motivations mean for vegetarian advocates? How can advocates use that information to get more people to go vegetarian?

First, a quick recap. Concern for animals and concern for health are by far the two main motivations people have for eating vegetarian. Among those aged twenty-five and under, concern for animals is the top motivation (although weight concerns are also important for some teenagers). Health takes precedence for those in their late forties and beyond.

Concern for the environment, disliking the taste of meat, and religious motivation all trail well behind in the 10 percent or under category. Environmental concerns are more important to younger vegetarians than older age groups. Only a small number of vegetarians, fewer than 2 percent, make the switch out of a concern for social justice or world hunger.

Health is by far the main motivation semi-vegetarians have for cutting back on meat or for not eating certain animal products. No other issue even comes close. However, semi-vegetarians who also care about animals or the environment are more likely to cut back on all types of meat, not just red meat.

Given this, what is the takeaway for those who would like to inspire as many people as possible to go vegetarian? Which messages should vegetarian advocates focus on in their conversations with friends, and in creating books, videos, fliers, and websites?

Let's go through each message one by one and make some informed guesses about how effective each message might be. Keep in mind: what follow aren't anything more than assumptions based on the data. The only way to actually find out which messages and message combinations work best is through controlled testing.

THE SOCIAL JUSTICE/WORLD HUNGER MESSAGE

Concern for social justice and world hunger motivates only a very small percentage of vegetarians. So it's probably not a very persuasive message for vegetarian advocates to use for inspiring people to stop eating meat.

(Wondering what the connection is between meat consumption and world hunger? Because farm animals eat a lot of grain, as meat consumption rises so does demand for grain. This sometimes pushes up the cost of grain, which puts a big burden on the global poor, since cheap grains are often their only source of food.)

Of course it's possible that few people go vegetarian for social justice reasons because few are aware of the connection between meat and global poverty. That's why only a controlled test could tell us how a social justice message actually stacks up against an animal welfare or health message.

The very fact that virtually no one is aware of the connection between social justice and vegetarianism, however, means it will probably be harder for people to understand, accept, and act on that message. It's easier for people to accept and act on messages that make immediate sense to them—like the idea that a vegetarian diet is healthier or kinder toward animals.

THE RELIGIOUS MESSAGE

If we look at vegetarians around the globe, religion and poverty are the two main reasons people don't eat meat. But in the industrialized world, only a minority of vegetarians are motivated by religious beliefs.

Using a religious message to encourage people to ditch meat might be helpful when targeting members of a religion with a history of vegetarianism, such as Buddhists or Seventh Day Adventists. On the other hand, if it were important to such believers that they strictly follow their religion, they would probably already be vegetarian. So it's possible that an animal- or health-focused message would be even more effective with devotees of a vegetarian-friendly faith. It would give them an additional reason to make the switch, instead of just reminding them about something they already knew.

It's also worth noting that, according to one study, people who are vegetarian for religious reasons are less likely to stick with it than people motivated by other concerns (Stahler, Retention Survey). However, a separate study discovered no difference in recidivism rates (Smith *et al.* 2000).

The bottom line is that, for the general public, a religious message will be very ineffective at getting people to go vegetarian. Advocates of vegetarian eating may want to target outreach toward members of a veg-friendly religion, but even with them it's anyone's guess as to whether a religious message or a health or animal welfare message will be more effective.

THE TASTE MESSAGE

For some vegetarians, disgust at the sight, smell, or taste of meat played a key role in getting them to change their diet. Taste seems to be just as important as environmental concerns in motivating people to go vegetarian.

Unfortunately, taste preferences aren't an easy route to persuasion. Taste is…well, a matter of taste! It's not something that can be easily changed by other people. The one thing vegetarian advocates might be able to do is evoke more revulsion toward meat by showing pictures of bloody steaks or other gristly meat products. Just what images are most likely to gross people out?

One study suggested that images of raw, uncooked meat increased disgust and made people less interested in eating at a particular restaurant. Giving the meat an animal's name increased aversion even more. The biggest increase in repulsion came from showing whole cuts of meat as opposed to meat on a plate, and from using images of red meat as opposed to white meat (Kubberod *et al.* 2008).

In general, people find red meat to be the most sickening of the mainstream meats. That's part of the reason why many consumers, especially women, prefer poultry. It has a more neutral odor and taste, and doesn't remind them of meat's bloody origins (Kubberod 2005). That raises the question of what happens when a person's abhorrence of meat increases, since if it caused them to shift from red meat to white meat, that would be bad news for animals.

But that's not necessarily what happens. A few studies suggest that aversion can lead people to cut back on all types of meat. Two studies found that people with more disgust toward meat ate it less often and enjoyed it less (Rousset *et al.* 2005; Ruby and

Heine 2012). One study found that including images of raw meat in fast food advertising increased feelings of antipathy for both beef and chicken (Kubberod *et al.* 2008). And media stories that make people turned off by meat can drive the public toward meat-free meals. When horsemeat was found in European beef and processed meat products in 2013, sales of vegetarian meats spiked (Butler).

It's also clear that repugnance at meat causes a lot of people to go fully vegetarian. At least one in ten vegetarians has ditched meat mainly because they don't like the taste of it. While not all of those people are actually disgusted by meat, studies show that many of them are (Santos and Booth 1996; Humane Research Council, Why or Why Not Vegetarian; Kubberod 2005; Beardsworth and Keil 1992; Greenebaum 2012). The demographic groups most likely to be revolted by meat are also the groups most likely to go vegetarian: women and young people (Kubberod 2005; Herzog and Golden 2009; Kubberod *et al.* 2008).

So will focusing on the repellent aspects of meat help vegetarian advocates inspire people to make a switch? It's possible. Stimulating disgust might make some people, particularly women and young people, slightly less interested in eating meat. But they'd need to be sure they weren't just driving people from red meat to poultry. So when going the aversion route, it might be good for vegetarian advocates to only use pictures of chicken.

In any case, highlighting the unpleasant aspects of meat will motivate only a small percentage of people to change their diet. It shouldn't be a main focus for those who are promoting vegetarian eating.

THE ENVIRONMENTAL MESSAGE

Most vegetarian advocates focus on three main reasons to go vegetarian: animals, health, and the environment. We know that concern for animals and concern for health are both major motivators of new vegetarians; the same can't be said for the environment.

If you ask people the main reason they went vegetarian, at most only 10 percent will say to protect the environment. Many studies have found the number to be well under 5 percent. Among semi-vegetarians, between zero and 15 percent say concern for the environment is their main reason for cutting back on meat.

As with the world hunger message, it's possible more people would go vegetarian for environmental reasons if they knew the impact meat has on the planet. Many people don't know that animal agriculture may be the largest source of greenhouse-gas emissions, or that producing meat requires dramatically more land and water than growing plant-based foods does. Most people are unaware that animal agriculture is the leading cause of water pollution and the second leading cause of air pollution in the U.S.

In a recent Swiss study, shoppers said they believed cutting back on meat does less good for the environment than buying food with minimal packaging, eating organic food, eating seasonal food, or eating local food (Tobler *et al.* 2011). A 2002 Humane Research Council study showed that even many vegetarians don't clearly understand the environmental impacts of eating meat (Humane Research Council, Focus Groups). A number of American and European studies have found that only a minority of the public thinks animal agriculture is a major cause of climate change (de Boer *et al.* 2013).

On the other hand, a recent Dutch study revealed two-thirds of the public had at least heard of the idea that eating meatless meals helps fight climate change. The more familiar people were with the idea, the more willing they were to eat less meat, and the more likely they were to already be cutting back (de Boer *et al.* 2013). In a Belgian study, consumers said that eating less meat was one of the most effective and practical ways to make their diet more sustainable (Vanhonacker *et al.* 2013).

All that being said, we should keep in mind that the environment isn't the only area where the public is unaware or dismissive of the impacts of eating vegetarian. One study found only a quarter of omnivores think a vegetarian diet is a healthier choice (60). Other studies have found similar results (Lea and Worsley 2003; Humane Research Council, Why or Why Not Vegetarian). An Australian study discovered that nearly half of the public thinks going vegetarian doesn't help animals (Lea, Moving From Meat). The lack of public awareness on the health and animal welfare issues hasn't stopped them from becoming the two main motivators for vegetarians.

Why isn't the environmental message inspiring more people to cut out meat? A couple of factors might make using it an uphill battle. First, as we saw earlier, people have a lot of other options when trying to "green" their life: they can buy locally produced food, seasonal food, food with less packaging, etc. Outside of the food realm they can drive less, reduce home energy use, recycle, and so forth. When it comes to helping the environment, it's easy for people to feel that they've already done their part and that they don't need to worry about meat.

When connecting meat consumption with climate change, another major barrier is that many people are skeptical about climate change. Only 50 percent of Americans, and only a slightly higher percentage of Europeans, believe climate change is occurring and is caused by human activity (Caldwell; Climate Change Opinion). So when vegetarian advocates point to climate change as a reason to go vegetarian, we've immediately lost half of our audience—although it's not quite as bad when we consider that climate change deniers tend to be from groups that are less likely to go vegetarian, such as older people and political conservatives.

A third drawback of the environmental message is that we don't see the direct harm we cause to the environment. Intellectually, we can understand that eating meat contributes to global warming, excess water usage, water pollution, and so forth. But we never see the direct impact of our own personal actions. We can see the chunk of dead animal on our plate and know we are responsible for his or her death. We can sense our own bodies and how healthful and energetic we are as a result of what we eat. The same can't be said for the environmental harm we cause by eating meat. Nearly all of it is out of sight. For what we can observe, such as extreme weather events caused by climate change, the problems will remain whether we eat meat or not.

Fourth, the production of red meat is often worse for the environment than poultry production. As a result, many environmental organizations encourage the public to switch from eating red meat to poultry. And as we know, that's bad news for animals. Vegetarian advocates can still focus on the environmental impacts of poultry production, and if they're using the environmental message they should. But a competing message about what meat to cut out in order to help the environment remains a problem.

A final drawback of the environmental message is that it's hard to tell stories about individuals. We humans evolved as a social species. Stories are incredibly powerful for shaping how we think about the world, what values we hold, and how we live our lives. In one study, people who were told a story about an individual starving child donated twice as much to help as people who were given facts about widespread hunger. In another study, people watching a persuasive speech were more than ten times more likely to remember stories than they were to remember particular facts (Cooney 2011).

It's easy to tell stories about the animal welfare or health benefits of eating a vegetarian diet. We can talk about an individual animal on a factory farm, or a person whose health improved after ditching meat. These stories might be part of the reason that videos of farm animal abuse often go viral online, reaching hundreds of thousands if not millions of viewers. Well-produced documentaries like *Forks Over Knives*, which profile people whose health improved dramatically after they changed their diet, have also been a hit. The same trend can be seen with wildly popular books such as Jonathan Safran Foer's *Eating Animals* and Rory Freedman and Kim Barnouin's *Skinny Bitch*.

It's much harder to tell a story about someone whose life was helped or harmed by the environmental impacts of meat production. Perhaps as a result, no video, book, or other media focused mainly on the environmental impacts of meat production has become very popular. Whatever the reason, the environmental message just doesn't seem to be as "sticky" as the health or animal messages.

At the end of the day, the environmental message still has some value. If as many as 10 percent of people who go vegetarian are doing so to protect the environment, that's a big enough group that they shouldn't be ignored. And it looks like the environmental motivation might be growing in popularity. Examining the studies listed in Chapter 7, we see that a 1989 study found just 1 percent of vegetarians were motivated by environmental concerns. That number rose to 4 percent in a 2002 study and to 9–10 percent in 2005 and 2012 studies.

Environmental concerns are also more popular among the group most likely to go vegetarian, young people (The TRU Study). An environmental message might be particularly effective when targeting audiences that care a lot about the environment, such as members of the Sierra Club or Greenpeace.

Here's the bottom line. The environmental message has some value, especially for young people and those who already identify as environmentalists. In the coming years it might become a much more common motivation for ditching meat. But at this point, even among young people, environmental concerns are much less likely than health or animal welfare concerns to inspire people to go vegetarian. Therefore the environmental message probably shouldn't be given equal attention when vegetarian advocates are encouraging the general public to cut out or cut back on meat.

THE ANIMAL WELFARE MESSAGE

Some vegetarians shy away from talking about the impacts of factory farming on animals. Perhaps they're health vegetarians who aren't really concerned with animals. Or maybe they think talking about farm animal issues will make people defensive or dismissive, which can certainly be the case. "Better to speak to people's self-interest," these vegetarian advocates say, "and focus only on the health benefits of ditching meat."

On average, you might get a more sympathetic ear by doing so. Most omnivores think the best reason to go vegetarian is to feel healthier. One study showed meat-eaters were four times more likely to report health as the best reason for eating vegetarian than they were to say protecting animals. Even saving money was seen as a better reason to go vegetarian than animal welfare (Roper Poll).

But here's the thing about what the general public thinks: it doesn't matter. Not very much, anyway. As vegetarian advocates, we're not trying to get people to nod their heads in agreement. We're trying to get as many individuals as possible to stop eating meat, or to at least eat less of it. If we want to know the best message for making that happen, we don't look to the people who haven't changed. We look to those who *have*, and we find out what moved them to do so. The issues that motivated them to stop eating meat should be the issues that compel other people to do the same.

Concern for animals is one of the two main reasons people go vegetarian. And for young people, the age group most likely to stop eating meat, concern for animals seems to be the top reason. It's also a particularly important spur for getting people to cut out eggs and dairy.

People who care a lot about animals may be slightly less likely to go back to eating meat. And while concern for animals is rarely the main reason people go semi-vegetarian, meat reducers who also care about animals are more likely to cut back on all types of meat, not just red meat.

Unless future research suggests otherwise, information about the depredations of animal agriculture should come standard when encouraging the public to ditch meat. Highlighting the cruelty done to farm animals will make advocates of vegetarian eating more effective in their work.

Vegetarian outreach focused on those under thirty should usually make animal cruelty the central message, while still including the health message. That focus may need to be reversed when targeting potential semi-vegetarians, or people over fifty, since most of them are motivated by health concerns. For the reasons outlined earlier though, vegetarian advocates will want to discuss the cruelty done to farm animals as well.

THE HEALTH MESSAGE

Concern for health is one of the two main reasons people go vegetarian. While it's a bit less important for those under thirty, a large percentage of young people do go vegetarian for health reasons.

Health is by far the most important impulse for semi-vegetarians. And as we saw earlier, semi-vegetarians are responsible for the majority of the drop in per capita U.S. meat consumption between 2006 and 2012. In other words, most of the fall in consumption was brought about by people eating less meat to improve their health.

Health vegetarians might eat a little more meat than ethical vegetarians. And those who don't care about animals might be slightly more likely to go back to eating meat. But the difference on both of these issues doesn't appear to be very large. As we found out earlier, many health vegetarians eventually accept the ethical reasons to stay meat-free.

If vegetarian advocates could wave a magic wand and create either an ethical vegetarian or a health vegetarian, they should probably lean toward creating an ethical one. But there are no such magic wands. And having people go vegetarian at all should be seen as what's most important.

As we noted, health is one of the two main reasons people go vegetarian and it's by far the main reason people go semi-vegetarian. It seems likely that many or most of those people would not have changed their diets for animal welfare reasons alone. So if vegetarian advocates want as many people as possible to ditch meat, and if they want anyone at all to cut back on the amount of meat they're eating, they should be sure to promote the health benefits of meat-free meals.

When they don't include the health message, vegetarian advocates risk missing many people they might have cajoled to go vegetarian. And they lose even more people they might have persuaded to cut back on meat.

When using the health message, advocates of vegetarian eating should keep a couple of pointers in mind. First, they should also talk about the cruelties that farm animals endure. Semi-vegetarians who care about both their health and farm animals eat fewer animals than those who only care about health. Vegetarians who care not just about health but also about animals may be slightly less likely to go back to eating meat. So the cruelty message needs to be included in vegetarian advocacy. Advocates should also try to educate current health vegetarians about the cruelty of animal agriculture.

Second—and this is extremely important—whenever they promote the health benefits of ditching meat, vegetarian advocates should focus specifically on chicken. They might also want to concentrate on farm-raised fish and eggs, the other two food groups that cause the most suffering. The health message that's presented should be that chicken, fish, and eggs have certain health risks, and that a diet free of chicken, fish, and eggs could have certain health benefits. If advocates just say that meat in general is unhealthful, or if they cite the health risks of red meat, they might inspire people to replace red meat with chicken—a net loss for animals.

Third, the general public doesn't necessarily have confidence in animal advocates when it comes to health information (Humane Research Council, Advocating Meat Reduction; Humane Research Council, Focus Groups). Doctors are the most trusted source on the health benefits of meat, followed by research reports (Heller; Humane Research Council, Focus Groups). Vegetarian advocates should utilize doctors, dietetic associations, and respectable research as their vehicles for highlighting the health reasons to go vegetarian. Because of these sources, the public will be more likely to trust the information and act on it.

(By the way, just what health concerns are causing people to cut out or cut back on meat? Most polls found a majority of respondents wanted a healthier diet in general. Weight worries were a primary reason for some, particularly semi-vegetarians. Concerns about antibiotics, additives, cancer, and diabetes also registered as important for a small number of people.)

The health messages that seem to have the most impact are those that highlight real-life consequences. For example, people need to know that they could lose weight, reduce their risk of heart disease, and have more energy if they cut out meat. It's less inspiring to hear that meat-free meals have fewer calories, less fat, and more vitamins and minerals (Wansink *et al.* 2005).

The bottom line is this: the health message is extremely important. A lot of people who go vegetarian, and the vast majority of people who start eating less meat, do so for health reasons. Their collective impact for animals is tremendously powerful. When encouraging the public to cut out or cut back on meat, advocates of vegetarian eating should make sure to highlight the health benefits of making a switch. The health message should focus on the potential health risks of chicken, fish, and eggs, and the potential benefits of taking those products off our plates.

CONCERNS WITH THE HEALTH MESSAGE

Some vegetarian advocates have concerns with the health message. They worry that it's an ineffective argument, and that it could hurt animals by driving people from red meat to poultry. Their argument against using the health message goes as follows:

First, advocates oversell veganism as by far the healthiest diet possible and a cure-all for every ailment, neither of which is true. Second, many people who try to go vegetarian eventually quit because they feel unhealthy. Third, the push to "eat healthy" has led people to eat less red meat and more chicken—a shift that has caused billions of additional farm animals to suffer. Fourth, the growing obesity epidemic illustrates that people don't pick what to eat based on health concerns. Fifth, connecting vegetarianism with healthful eating has led producers and restaurants to label vegetarian food as "healthy," a label that turns off most consumers. Sixth, the health message hasn't been effective at increasing the number of vegetarians. Seventh, the health message just encourages people to care about themselves, whereas an ethical message hastens the day when society treats animals with compassion.

Most of these points make intuitive sense. But after looking at all the data, many of these criticisms evaporate. The few that remain serve as pointers on *how* to use the health message, not as arguments against employing it. Let's go through each point briefly.

First, overselling veganism as a miraculous diet is certainly a bad idea. Even vegan dietitians say the jury is still out as to whether a vegan, vegetarian, or pescatarian diet is the most healthful. But meat-free eating does have proven health benefits. Vegetarian advocates can point out those benefits without making wild claims.

Chicken, fish, and eggs—the foods that cause the most animal suffering—also have scientifically demonstrated health risks. For example, chicken and eggs are two of the biggest sources of saturated fat intake. That's one reason they are linked to higher death rates from breast cancer. And chicken and fish have elevated levels of cancer-causing chemicals such as dioxin, arsenic, and mercury.

Advocates of vegetarian eating can and should point those facts out to the public. There is nothing inaccurate or difficult about highlighting these risks and encouraging the public to move away from those products. And vegetarian advocates can do so without making the broad claim that a vegan diet is the healthiest diet possible. They don't even have to make the general claim that a diet free of chicken or fish is definitively better for you than a diet containing those products.

Second, it's true that many people who go vegetarian later go back to eating meat because they felt unhealthy. But that happens to *both* health and ethical vegetarians, who appear to have similar recidivism rates. There's no evidence that one group is more likely than the other to backslide for health reasons. One study looked at a group of former vegetarians, the majority of whom had initially ditched meat for ethical reasons. Their main reason for returning to meat? They felt unhealthy as vegetarians (Herzog 2011). So changing the message won't change the percentage of vegetarians going back to meat. What will help is showing all new vegetarians how to be healthy, and in particular where to get protein and iron.

Third, it's true that the general push for healthy eating in the U.S. has contributed to skyrocketing poultry consumption. Declining poultry prices have also played a major role. But that push for healthy eating will continue full speed whether vegetarian advocates enter the conversation or not. And if they don't, the only message the public will continue to hear ad nauseam is that healthy eating means eating less red meat and more chicken and fish. If vegetarian advocates do engage in the public-health conversation, they can introduce a new message: chicken (and fish, and eggs, and other meat) has health risks, and removing them has potential health benefits.

On a more basic level, we should note that encouraging the public to "eat healthy" and encouraging the public to "cut out chicken, fish, and other meat to improve your health" are two different messages. As such, they will likely produce different results. Encouraging people to eat less chicken should lead some people to do so. It is supremely unlikely that pointing out the health risks of chicken consumption, and directly and repeatedly encouraging people to cut out or cut back on chicken, is going to lead people to eat more chicken than they did before. Numerous health studies make clear that when you point out the health risks of a certain food, if the public changes at all it's usually to move away from that food (Davidow).

Fourth, the idea that health concerns don't influence what people eat is untrue.

As we just discussed, red meat consumption has declined because of health concerns. And between 2006 and 2012, all meat consumption—including chicken—declined by a whopping 10 percent. This collapse was due in large part to the growing number of semi-vegetarians. And what was their primary reason for cutting back on meat? Health concerns.

Sure, most Americans don't pursue a healthful diet. But most Americans also don't pursue an animal-friendly diet. Nevertheless, the surveys cited in Chapter 7 make clear that both the animal welfare and the health message inspire some percentage of people to stop eating meat.

Fifth, it's true that labeling vegetarian food as "healthy" can turn off some mainstream consumers. Research is mixed though; sometimes a health label actually increases sales (Horgen and Brownell 2002; Wansink *et al.* 2000). At any rate, the world is very different today than it was twenty years ago. Back then, only small health-food stores carried specialty vegetarian food. Today vegetarian options are everywhere, including mainstream grocery stores and fast-food chains. None of the major vegetarian meat companies label their products as "healthy," nor do most restaurants. Vegetarian advocates are free to point out the potential health benefits of going meat-free, and then provide mouth-watering meal suggestions that are not labeled as "healthy." And if they want to be effective, vegetarian advocates should indeed refrain from telling new vegetarians to fill up on quinoa and sprouts.

Sixth, it's simply not true that the health message has been ineffective at increasing the number of vegetarians. As we've seen, health is one of the main reasons people cut out meat and it is by far the lead reason people cut back on meat. This is true despite the fact that there is only one well-funded group—the Physicians Committee for Responsible Medicine—that uses only the health message to promote vegan eating. Movies like *Forks Over Knives* and books like *Skinny Bitch* and *The China Study* have helped fill that organizational gap. These and other titles have used the health message to drive large numbers of people toward vegetarian eating. As we've mentioned several times, it is the perceived health benefits of cutting back on meat that have led to the large drop in U.S. meat consumption between 2006 and 2012.

Seventh, it's true that the health argument promotes only self-interest and not a wider concern for animals. Ultimately, we would all like to steer public opinion toward compassion for animals. But as we saw, many health vegetarians go on to adopt concern for farm animals as a primary or additional reason for staying meat-free. Many would never have gone vegetarian in the first place, and therefore never come to care about farm animals, if not for the health message.

In the end, it's people's behavior that impacts animals and not their attitudes. If attitudes were what mattered, farm animal welfare would be honored much more. As many as 97 percent of Americans say they think farm animals should be protected from cruelty, and 25 percent say they think animals should have the exact same protection from harm as human beings (Newport, Post-Derby Tragedy). Many people already hold the attitude towards animals that vegetarian advocates want them to possess. The question is how to get those people—and everyone else—to change their behavior. One health vegetarian who cares nothing about animals will probably spare more animal suffering in their lifetime than a hundred self-described animal lovers who continue to eat meat.

If vegetarian advocates want to help as many animals as possible, they should usually include the health message alongside the animal welfare message in their outreach. There are certainly some do's and don'ts when it comes to using the health message. But the data strongly suggest that it is one of the most powerful tools advocates have for sparing farm animals a lifetime of misery.

A FINAL WORD ON MOTIVATIONS

In this chapter, we've assumed that the best way to understand what messages will inspire people to ditch meat is to look at current vegetarians and semi-vegetarians and see what inspired them to make a change. But what we've been working off of is just that: an assumption. Since most people who go vegetarian do so to improve their health or protect animals, we've assumed that those are the most effective messages for getting others to change as well. That may not be the case.

The problem is we don't know how often the public is hearing each message. For example, let's say that over the course of their life the average person reads lots of news articles, watches many news reports, and hears their friends talk about how going vegetarian will save animals. Much less often, they hear the idea that going vegetarian will improve their health. If there were equal numbers of health vegetarians and ethical vegetarians in the country, it would suggest that the health message is actually more powerful. But we have no idea how many times the public hears each type of message, or how it's communicated to them.

The only way to really know which message is most effective is through controlled testing. Outreach materials with different messages would need to be given out to similar audiences. Researchers would then need to follow up with each audience to see which group changed their diet the most.

So far, only one study has taken a taken a crack at doing just that. A 2012 Humane Research Council study showed viewers between the ages of fifteen and twenty-three videos related to vegetarianism. One video focused exclusively on the cruelty done to farm animals. A second had some cruelty footage but was primarily a happy story about a rescued farm animal. A third discussed the environmental reasons to go vegan. And the fourth told the story of a couple who had gone vegan for health reasons. Each person watched just one video. They were then asked how interested they were in removing animal products from their diet.

Of those who watched the cruelty video 48 percent said they would consider reducing or eliminating animal products. Only 37–39 percent of those who watched one of the other three videos said the same. The results suggest that focusing on animal cruelty is the most effective message to use when targeting young people (Veg-Fund Video Survey).

As you might remember, concern for animals is also the main reason young people go vegetarian. So this one study seems to bear out our assumption: the most common reason for being vegetarian among a particular demographic group is probably the most effective message to use for getting other members of that group to go vegetarian.

Of course, this one study isn't proof that an animal cruelty message is the most effective message to use with young people. Like any study, this one had its limitations. The studied group was a captive audience, which is not usually the case when conducting vegetarian advocacy. The videos were produced by different organizations, so some were much more polished than others. And the study didn't measure how much people actually changed their diet, only how willing they were to change it. It also didn't use any videos with combination messages, for example a video that included both the health and animal cruelty reasons.

Limitations aside, it's studies like this that will show which messages are really most effective at inspiring dietary change and sparing the lives of farm animals. Humane League Labs, a research project run by The Humane League, began a string of studies like this one in 2013 to provide more much-needed data. I hope that other vegetarian advocacy organizations will conduct similar research in the coming years.

15

INSPIRING CHANGE

A RESEARCH-BASED CHECKLIST ON WHAT WILL MOTIVATE THE PUBLIC TO DITCH MEAT

THIS BOOK WAS WRITTEN FOR TWO REASONS. FIRST, TO BE an interesting and at times entertaining look at who vegetarians are and what makes them tick; secondly, and more seriously, to share research that would enable vegetarian advocates to be more effective in their work.

With that in mind, let's finish with a nutshell review of what the research can teach advocates of vegetarian eating. By basing their work on facts and not philosophies, their advocacy will be more effective at steering the public toward cruelty-free eating. By employing data and not assumptions, they will be more effective at sparing farm animals a lifetime of misery.

THE CAVEATS

Please keep in mind that this book isn't a bible. The pointers below are based on the best data we have at the moment and not eternal truths. Future research will probably show at least a few of them to be wrong. Also keep in mind that what follow are general guidelines, not rigid rules. Approaches that don't work well in general might work in certain situations and with certain audiences. Virtually all of the research we've cited comes from the U.S., Canada, Australia, and Europe. As a result, some of the recommendations might not be effective in other parts of the world. Lastly, the only way to get direct guidance is to do direct research. Some of the studies in this book fit that description. For example, studies by the Humane Research Council, The Humane League, and Farm Sanctuary offer concrete information on which vegetarian advocacy videos and leaflets are most effective. Some of them also give a sense of how effective vegetarian advocacy programs are overall. These are the most important and most useful studies. They present firm guidance about what vegetarian advocates should do to create as much dietary change as possible.

But most of the studies we've covered in this book provide only indirect evidence about what will work best. For example, the data suggest that using both an animal welfare and a health message will inspire more people to go vegetarian than using only an animal welfare message. But we don't know that for sure. The sooner that vegetarian advocacy organizations or researchers carry out direct research on these types of questions, the better off advocates—and animals—will be.

Okay, you've been fully warned! Without further ado, here are some research-based recommendations for those who advocate vegetarian eating.

KEY RECOMMENDATIONS FROM RESEARCH ON VEGETARIANS

Animals Impacted

- Focus on getting people to cut out or cut back on chicken, fish, and eggs. Explain to them why that is the best place to start when changing your diet. Chickens (both meat and egg-laying) and fish account for 92 percent of the farm animals killed for food in the U.S. They also represent 95 percent of the days of animal suffering caused each year by omnivores.
- Refrain from talking about the health risks of red meat. Also refrain from encouraging people to cut back on red meat or to simply "eat healthy."
- Point out that even eating less meat, especially less chicken and fish, is a good thing. Meat reducers are sparing hundreds of millions of animals each year from a life of misery.
- Be aware that most people who call themselves vegetarian still eat meat. Encourage self-identified vegetarians to continue cutting out animal products, especially chicken, fish, and eggs.

Audience

- Focus vegetarian advocacy on those people most likely to change their diet. Women and young people—and in particular young women—are most likely to cut out or cut back on meat. Just by concentrating on them you can double or triple the number of animals you spare with your vegetarian advocacy.
- When possible, target young women who are particularly likely to go vegetarian. Those who are Democrats, single, smart, not following Judeo-Christian religions,

artistic, LGBT, introverts, or living in large cities should be more likely to ditch meat.

- Keep in mind which groups eat the most animals. For example, African-Americans eat far more animals than other ethnic groups.

Barriers

- Help the public overcome the main barriers to going vegetarian. Show them that meat-free food can be delicious. Give them pointers on how to be healthy as a vegetarian, with particular emphasis on how to get iron and protein. Also teach them the easiest ways to make and find vegetarian meals, including when eating with friends.
- Focus as much on *how* to go vegetarian as you do on the reasons for making the switch. This will assist people in making the transition. Offer them helpful resources like vegetarian starter guides and links to vegetarian eating websites.
- Provide social support for new vegetarians. Also, once people have already gone vegetarian, help them see their diet as a part of who they are. Both of these should make people more likely to stay vegetarian.

The Minds of Animals

- Point out that farm animals feel physical and psychological pain, and that they have complex, human-like emotions. This will make people less comfortable with eating meat.
- Describe farm animals in human-like ways. Give them specific names and talk about them as you would about a human being. Use photos that emphasize those human-like qualities.
- Include images of cute animals as well as images of animals who are suffering.

Motivations

- Emphasize the animal welfare reasons to cut out or cut back on meat. Use this message with both potential vegetarians and with current vegetarians and semi-vegetarians. The more that people care about animals, even if it's not their main motivation for being vegetarian, the fewer animals they will eat. Concern for animals is also one of the main reasons people go vegetarian.
- Include a health message focused on the potential health risks of chicken, fish, and eggs, and the benefits of meat-free meals. Show the real-life benefits people experience from going meat-free. Use quotes from doctors and reputable health organizations. People's main concerns are their overall health, though you might

also touch on weight, antibiotics, additives, food safety, cancer, and diabetes. Concern for health is one of the main reasons people go vegetarian, and it is the main reason people cut back on the amount of meat they're eating.

- Refrain from focusing on religious and social justice/world hunger reasons to go vegetarian, except possibly among specific audiences. Also don't place too much stress on the environmental reasons to go meat-free, except among specific audiences. If using disgust to try to motivate your audience, be sure to focus on the sickening aspects of chicken, fish, and eggs.

The Switch

- Advise people to change their diet gradually rather than abruptly. This should make them more likely to go and stay vegetarian.
- Encourage people to try tasty vegan meats, in particular the most meat-like chicken products, sausages, burgers, patties, and nuggets.
- Refrain from suggesting to people that they try lots of foods that are brand new to them, or foods that they may consider extremely healthful. These include new and unusual grains, vegetables, meal combinations, and ethnic dishes.
- Persuade people to cut out or cut back on meat, or to go "meat-free," instead of urging them to go vegetarian or vegan.
- Use appetizing descriptive language when labeling a vegetarian meal.

Testing and Research

- If you work with a vegetarian advocacy organization, carry out direct testing as much as possible to see which approaches work best. Share your results with other organizations. Base your decisions about what to do and how to do it on research.

KEY RECOMMENDATIONS FROM GENERAL SOCIAL-PSYCHOLOGY RESEARCH

The recommendations below are based on research that wasn't covered in this book. They come from general social-psychology research, most of which was discussed in my book *Change of Heart: What Psychology Can Teach Us About Spreading Social Change* (Cooney 2011). For the research behind these tips, please check out *Change of Heart*. While this research wasn't done on vegetarians, the results are very useful for vegetarian advocacy.

- Write vegetarian advocacy materials at a sixth-grade reading level. This helps people understand and remember the information (Readability of Vegan Outreach Literature).

- Use stories about individual animals or people. Stories stick in people's memories, and are more persuasive than facts or figures.

- Use "social norms" messages. Tell people that millions of Americans have gone vegetarian and that Americans are eating less and less meat each year. Mention celebrities who have gone vegetarian. Social norms messages are extremely effective at getting people to change their behavior.

- Use images of conventionally attractive, fit, and happy individuals who are excited to be eating vegetarian. Research shows these images make your message more persuasive.

- Portray vegetarian men as very masculine in order to counter stereotypes.

- Connect vegetarian eating with generic values that your audience endorses. Those values might include patriotism, freedom, generalized religious notions, the quest for self-improvement, and the pursuit of happiness (Allen *et al.* 2008; Tukker *et al.* 2008).

- Make clear to people that ditching meat is a choice and that the decision is up to them. People are more likely to change once their freedom to choose has been reaffirmed (The One [Really Easy] Persuasion Technique).

- Use quotes from doctors, scientists, veterinarians, dietary organizations, major newspapers, and magazines. Messages are more persuasive when they come from people who are perceived as authorities.

- Encourage people to set a specific goal for how they'll change. When possible, have them make some type of commitment. Both of these will make people more likely to follow through.

- Use fairly graphic imagery of animals suffering. The images shouldn't be so explicit that most people turn away and miss the message about what they can do to help. Graphic imagery, when accompanied by a message about how to help, makes people more likely to change.

- Keep your information short and repeat a common theme. Avoid overloading people with facts. This will help them absorb your message.

- Point out to people that ditching meat is in line with who they already are and what they already believe. Also show that it fits in with who they want to be. People are more likely to make a change when that change meshes with how they view themselves.

- Refrain from guilt-tripping people. Guilt-based messages make people less likely to change. It's not problematic if they feel guilty when they find out how animals are treated, but you don't want to directly tell them it's their fault.

- Inform people about the number of animals they'll save by cutting out or cutting back on meat. People are more likely to do something when they know it will have concrete results.

- Design vegetarian advocacy materials with an attractive style and font to make your message more persuasive.

- Use emotional and not philosophical arguments. Philosophical arguments are much less persuasive for most people.

- Focus on changing people's behavior, not just their attitude. For many people, there is a big gap between their attitude and their behavior. Animals won't be helped unless people change their behavior.

- Refrain from repeating and then dispelling myths about vegetarian eating. Many people will become confused and misremember the myths as truths.

- Don't tell people in advance what you are trying to persuade them to do. Get them interested in what you are saying first. People who know in advance what you're trying to persuade them of will immediately start coming up with counterarguments.

- Encourage people to make a change that is significant but that they could probably picture themselves doing. Requests like this lead to the largest amount of behavioral change.

- Use the approaches and messaging that will create the most change and help the greatest number of animals. Refrain from simply sticking with the approaches that are easiest for you, or the messages that most perfectly express what you believe.

CONCLUSION

IF YOU'VE MADE IT TO THE END OF THIS BOOK, YOU'RE probably someone who really cares about animals. You know they suffer lives of intense misery on modern farms. You want to do what you can to help end that suffering.

Replacing animal products with something non-animal-based is the first step that many people take. If you've already gone in that direction, wonderful! I hope that learning a little more about the suffering farm animals go through has inspired you to leave all animal products (and in particular chicken, farm-raised fish, and eggs) off your plate. If you're already vegan, congratulations! It's also my hope that the research in this book will help you stick with it for the rest of your life.

Cutting animal products out of your diet is the first step to combating cruelty, but you don't have to stop there. By encouraging other people to adopt the same compassionate diet, you can double, triple, even quadruple the number of animals you help over the course of your life. By becoming an advocate for vegetarian eating you can go from sparing hundreds of animals in your lifetime to sparing hundreds of thousands.

Every farm animal values his or her life and happiness like we value ours. Every one is as smart, playful, affectionate, kind, and unique as the cat curled up on our windowsill or the dog at the foot of our bed. Is there any better use of your time, your money, or your energy than working to spare these individuals from a lifetime of pain?

Compassionate people like you are the only hope animals have of escaping existential misery. That is not a theory or poetic rhetoric. It's a cold, hard fact. Thousands of animals will suffer or not suffer based on the choices you make. Those who truly care about animals will do all they can to reduce as much animal suffering as possible.

Because farm animals suffer so tremendously, advocates of vegetarian eating need to bring their "A" game to the table. For too long, the vegetarian advocacy movement has shot blindly in the dark. For too long, it has relied on hunches and anecdotes to guide its choices. For too long, it has looked at the scientific method and said, *No, thanks. That doesn't apply to changing behavior.* More often, the thought of using a research-based approach hasn't even crossed the minds of vegetarian advocates.

Meanwhile leaders in every other field, from sales to technology to politics to education, have turned to hard data to better reach their goals. Animals deserve at least that much diligence. Animals deserve at least that much professionalism.

The sooner vegetarian advocates put the research that already exists to use, the more animals will be spared their misery. The sooner vegetarian advocates carry out direct research to guide their decisions, the closer we will all be to the world we want to see.

WORKS CITED

Allen, M. *Social Structure, Status Seeking and the Basic Food Groups.* ANZMAC 2005 Conference: Consumer Behavior. Perth: Australian and New Zealand Marketing Academy, 2005.

Allen, M. A., Gupta, R., and A. Monnier. "The Interactive Effect of Cultural Symbols and Human Values on Taste Evaluation." *Journal of Consumer Research* 35.2 (2008):294–308.

Allen, M. W., and S. Baines. "Manipulating the Symbolic Meaning of Meat to Encourage Greater Acceptance of Fruits and Vegetables and Less Proclivity for Red and White Meat." *Appetite* 38 (2002):118–130.

Allen, M. W., Wilson, M., Ng, S. H., and M. Dunne. "Values and Beliefs of Vegetarians and Omnivores." *The Journal of Social Psychology* 140.4 (2000):405–422.

AllRecipes. *The Measuring Cup.* AllRecipes, 2011. PDF file. Web. <http://press.allrecipes.com/wp-content/uploads/Allrecipes_2011TrendsReport.pdf>

"Americans Pick Ronald McDonald Over Burger King for President." *Public Policy Polling.* 26 Feb 2013. 1 Mar 2013. <http://www.publicpolicypolling.com/pdf/2011/PPP_Release_NationalFOOD_022613.pdf>

"Americans Say Food Production Headed in Right Direction, Widespread Misperceptions Remain." *PR Newswire.* 15 Nov 2012. 1 Mar 2013. <http://www.prnewswire.com/news-releases/americans-say-food-production-headed-in-right-direction-widespread-misperceptions-remain-179465971.html>

Anderson, A. S., and S. E. Morris. "Changing Fortunes: Changing Food Choices." *Nutrition & Food Science* 30.1 (2000):12–15.

Armitage, C. J. "Can Variables from the Transtheoretical Model Predict Dietary Change?" *Journal of Behavioral Medicine* 33 (2010):264–273.

Armstrong, J. B., and M. E. Hutchins. "Development of an Attitude to Measure Attitudes Toward Humans' Use of Nonhuman Animals." *Perceptual and Motor Skills* 82 (1996):1003–1010.

Arppe, T., Makela, J., and V. Vaananen. "Living Food Diet and Veganism: Individual vs. Collective Boundaries of the Forbidden." *Social Science Information* 50.2 (2011):275–297.

Aston, L. M., Smith, J. N., and J. W. Powles. "Meat Intake in Britain in Relation to Other Dietary Components and to Demographic and Risk Factor Variables: Analyses Based on the National Diet and Nutrition Survey of 2000/2001." *Journal of Human Nutrition and Dietetics* 26 (2012):96–106.

Back, K. W., and M. Glasgow. "Social Networks and Psychological Conditions in Diet Preferences: Gourmets and Vegetarians." *Basic and Applied Social Psychology* 2.1 (1981):1–9.

Baines, S., Powers, J., and W. J. Brown. "How Does the Health and Well-Being of Young Australian Vegetarian and Semi-Vegetarian Women Compare with Non-Vegetarians?" *Public Health Nutrition* 10.5 (2007):436–442.

Baker, S., Thompson, K. E., and D. Palmer-Barnes. "Crisis in the Meat Industry: A Values-Based Approach to Communications Strategy." *Journal of Marketing Communications* 8.1 (2002):19–30.

Barahal, M. "The Cruel Vegetarian." *Psychiatric Quarterly* 20.1 (1946):3S–13S.

Barclay, E. "Why There's Less Red Meat on Many American Plates." *NPR*. 27 Jun 2012. 1 Mar 2013. <http://www.npr.org/blogs/thesalt/2012/06/27/155837575/why-theres-less-red-meat-served-on-many-american-plates>

Barr, S. I., and G. E. Chapman. "Perceptions and Practices of Self-Defined Current Vegetarian, Former Vegetarian, and Nonvegetarian Women." *Journal of the American Dietetic Association* 102.3 (2002):354–360.

Barr, S. I., Janelle, K. C., and J. C. Prior. "Vegetarian vs. Nonvegetarian Diets, Dietary Restraint, and Subclinical Ovulatory Disturbances: Prospective 6-mo Study." *American Journal of Clinical Nutrition* 60.6 (1994):887–894.

Bas, M., Karabudak, E., and G. Kiziltan. "Vegetarianism and Eating Disorders: Association Between Eating Attitudes and Other Psychological Factors among Turkish Adolescents." *Appetite* 44 (2005):309–315.

Bastian, B., Loughnan, S., Haslam, N., and H. R. M. Radke. "Don't Mind Meat? The Denial of Mind to Animals Used for Human Consumption." *Personality and Social Psychology Bulletin* 38.2 (2012):247–256.

Beardsworth, A. and A. Bryman. "Meat Consumption and Meat Avoidance Among Young People." *British Food Journal* 106.4 (2004):313–327.

——. "Meat Consumption and Vegetarianism Among Young Adults in the UK." *British Food Journal* 101.4 (1999):289–300.

Beardsworth, A., and T. Keil. "Health-Related Beliefs and Dietary Practices Among Vegetarians and Vegans: A Qualitative Study." *Health Education Journal* 50.1 (1991):38–42.

——. "The Vegetarian Option: Varieties, Conversions, Motives and Careers." *The Sociological Review* 40 (1992):253–293.

Beardsworth, A. D., and E. T. Keil. "Contemporary Vegetarianism in the U.K.: Challenge and Incorporation?" *Appetite* 20 (1993):229–234.

——. "Vegetarianism, Veganism, and Meat Avoidance: Recent Trends and Findings." *British Food Journal* 93.4 (1991):19–24.

Beardsworth, A., Bryman, A., Keil, A., Goode, J., Haslam, C., and E. Lancashire. "Women, Men and Food: The Significance of Gender for Nutritional Attitudes and Choices." *British Food Journal* 104.7 (2002):470–491.

Beezhold, B. L., and C. S. Johnston. "Restriction of Meat, Fish, and Poultry in Omnivores Improves Mood: A Pilot Randomized Controlled Trial." *Nutrition Journal* 11.9 (2012).

Berndsen, M., and J. van der Pligt. "Ambivalence Toward Meat." *Appetite* 42 (2004):71–78.

Bilewicz, M., Imhoff, R., and M. Drogosz. "The Humanity of What We Eat: Conceptions of Human Uniqueness Among Vegetarians and Omnivores." *European Journal of Social Psychology* 41 (2011):201–209.

Bill and Melinda Gates Foundation. *Annual Letter from Bill Gates, 2013.* PDF file, 2013. Web. 1 Mar 2013. <http://annualletter.gatesfoundation.org/#nav=section1&slide=0>

Blake, M. L. "'I Don't Like Meat to Look Like Animals': How Consumer Behavior Responds to Animal Rights Campaigns." Diss. Marylhurst University, 2008. Web. 1 Mar 2013.

Bobic, J., Cvijetic, S., Baric, I. C., and Z. Satalic. "Personality Traits, Motivation and Bone Health in Vegetarians." *Collegium Antropologicum* 36.3 (2012):795–800.

Bosman, M. J. C., Ellis, S. M., Bouwer, S. C., Jerling, J. C., Erasmus, A. C., Harmse, N., and J. Badham. "South African Consumers' Opinions and Consumption of Soy and Soy Products." *International Journal of Consumer Studies* 33 (2009):425–435.

Boyle, D. "Becoming Vegetarian: An Analysis of the Vegetarian Career Using an Integrated Model of Deviance." Diss. Virginia Polytechnic Institute, 2007. Web. 1 Mar 2013.

Boyle, J. E. "Becoming Vegetarian: The Eating Patterns and Accounts of Newly Practicing Vegetarians." *Food and Foodways: Explorations in the History and Culture of Human Nourishment* 19 (2011):314–333.

Bratanova, B., Loughnan, S., and B. Bastian. "The Effect of Categorization as Food on the Perceived Moral Standing of Animals." *Appetite* 57 (2011):193–196.

"Broiler." Wikipedia. 2013. 1 Mar 2013. <http://www.en.wikipedia.org/wiki/Broiler>

Butler, S. "Horsemeat Scandal Sparks Rise in Sales of Vegetarian Alternatives." *The Guardian.* 5 Mar 2013. Web. 10 Mar 2013. <http://www.guardian.co.uk/uk/2013/mar/05/horsemeat-scandal-sales-vegetarian-alternatives>

Butterfield, M. E., Hill, S. E., and C. G. Lord. "Mangy Mutt or Furry Friend? Anthropomorphism Promotes Animal Welfare." *Journal of Experimental Social Psychology* 48 (2012):957–960.

Byrd-Bredbenner, C., Grenci, A., and V. Quick. "Effect of a Television Programme on Nutrition Cognitions and Intended Behaviours." *Nutrition & Dietetics* 67 (2010):143–149.

Caldwell, M. "Poll: Most Americans Believe in Man-Made Climate Change." *Mother Jones.* 20 Oct 2012. 1 Mar 2013. <http://www.motherjones.com/blue-marble/2012/10/americans-are-finally-warming-climate-change>

"Calories in Food." *FreeDieting.* 2012. 1 Mar 2013. <http://www.freedieting.com/tools/calories_in_food.htm>

Castano, E., and R. Giner-Sorolla. "Not Quite Human: Infrahumanization in Response to Collective Responsibility for Intergroup Killing." *Journal of Personality and Social Psychology* 90 (2006):804–818.

Chapman, N. *Where Is the Soyfood Market Headed.* Third Annual Soyfoods Symposium Proceedings, 1998. PDF file.

"Checkoff Tracks Activist Groups' Influence on Kids." *Pork Checkoff.* 2007. 1 Mar 2013. <http://www.pork.org/News/645/Feature325.aspx#.TyIMAeNWoyc>

Childers, M. A., Herzog, H., and B. Railsback. "Motivations for Meat Consumption Among Ex-Vegetarians." *Council on Undergraduate Research.* 2009. 1 Mar 2013. <https://ncurdb.cur.org/ncur/archive/Display_NCUR.aspx?id=20526>

Chilton, S. M., Burgess, D., and W. G. Hutchinson. "The Relative Value of Farm Animal Welfare." *Ecological Economics* 59 (2006):353–363.

Chin, M. G., Fisak, Jr., B., and V. K. Sims. "Development of the Attitudes Toward Vegetarians Scale." *Anthrozoös* 15.4 (2002):332–342.

Chlebowski, G. "Vegetarian Resource Group Survey Results from Veggie Fest, Naperville, IL, August 8–9, 2009." *Vegetarian Resource Group.* 2009. 1 Mar 2013. <http://www.vrg.org/nutshell/veggiefest_poll_09.php>

Cialdini, R., Brown, S., Lewis, B., Luce, C., and S. Neuberg. "Reinterpreting The Empathy–Altruism Relationship: When One Into One Equals Oneness." *Journal of Personality and Social Psychology* 73 (1997):481–494.

"Climate Change Opinion by Country." Wikipedia. 2013. 1 Mar 2013. <http://www.en.wikipedia.org/wiki/Climate_change_opinion_by_country>

Cole, M., and K. Morgan. "Vegaphobia: Derogatory Discourses of Veganism and the Reproduction of Speciesism in UK National Newspapers." *The British Journal of Sociology* 62.1 (2011):134–153.

"Consumers Prefer 'Meat-Free' to Vegetarian." *The Telegraph* 5 Feb 2008. Web. 1 Mar 2013. <http://www.telegraph.co.uk/news/uknews/1577631/Consumers-prefer-meat-free-to-vegetarian.html>

"Consumers Rate Chicken on Ten Attributes." *Humane Research Council.* 2 Feb 2007. 1 Mar 2013. <http://www.humanespot.org/content/consumers-rate-chicken-ten-attributes>

Cooney, N. *Change of Heart: What Psychology Can Teach Us About Spreading Social Change.* New York: Lantern Books, 2011.

——."The Powerful Impact of College Leafleting Part 1." *Farm Sanctuary.* 15 Jan 2013. 1 Mar 2013. <http://ccc.farmsanctuary.org/the-powerful-impact-of-college-leafleting-part-1/>

Cooper, C. K., Wise, T. N., and L. S. Mann. "Psychological and Cognitive Characteristics of Vegetarians." *Psychosomatics* 26.6 (1985):521–527.

Corliss, Richard. "Should We All Be Vegetarians?" *Time* magazine, 15 July 2002. Web. 1 Mar 2013. <http://www.time.com/time/magazine/article/0,9171,1002888,00.html>

Cronin, J. M., McCarthy, M. B., and A. M. Collins. "Covert Distinction: How Hipsters Practice Food-Based Resistance Strategies in the Production of Identity." *Consumption Markets & Culture* (2012):1–27.

Curtis, M. J., and L. K. Comer. "Vegetarianism, Dietary Restraint, and Feministy Identity." *Eating Behaviors* 7 (2006):91–104.

Daniel, C. R., Cross, A. J., Koebnick, C., and R. Sinha. "Trends in Meat Consumption in the United States." *Public Health Nutrition* 14.4 (2011):575–583.

Davidow, B. "Hypothesis: Increasing the Availability of Evidence that Meat is Bad for Your Health Will Decrease Red Meat Consumption (Beef, Pork) and Increase White Meat Consumption (Chicken, Fish)." 2012. PDF file.

de Boer, J., and H. Aiking. "On the Merits of Plant-Based Proteins for Global Food Security: Marrying Macro and Micro Perspectives." *Ecological Economics* 70 (2011):1259–1265.

de Boer, J., Boersema, J. J., and H. Aiking. "Consumers' Motivational Associations Favoring Free-Range Meat or Less Meat." *Ecological Economics* 68 (2009):850–860.

de Boer, J., Hoogland, C. T., and J. J. Boersema. "Toward More Sustainable Food Choices: Value Priorities and Motivational Orientations." *Food Quality and Preference* 18 (2007):985–996.

de Boer, J., Schosler, H., and J. J. Boersema. "Climate Change and Meat Eating: An Inconvenient Couple?" *Journal of Environmental Psychology* 33 (2013):1–8.

——. "Motivational Differences in Food Orientation and the Choice of Snacks Made from Lentils, Locusts, Seaweed, or 'Hybrid' Meat." *Food Quality and Preference* 28 (2013):32–35.

De Houwer, J., and E. De Bruycker. "Implicit Attitudes Toward Meat and Vegetables in Vegetarians and Nonvegetarians." *International Journal of Psychology* 42.3 (2007):158–165.

"Demographics of the United States." Wikipedia. 2013. 1 Mar 2013. <http://en.wikipedia.org/wiki/Demographics_of_the_United_States#Race_and_ethnicity?>

Department of Applied Sciences, Department of Agricultural Economics, University of Missouri–Columbia. *2011 U.S. Meat and Poultry Consumption and Demand: The Facts*. DASS, DAE, UM-C, 2012. PDF file.

Dietz, T., Frisch, A. S., Kalof, L., Stern, P. C., and G. A. Guagnano. "Values and Vegetarianism: An Exploratory Analysis." *Rural Sociology* 60.3 (1995):533–542.

Dillard, C. "Strategic Communication for Animal Activists." *Humane Research Council*. 31 May 2011. 1 Mar 2013. <http://www.humanespot.org/content/strategic-communication-animal-activists>

"Do You Consider Yourself a Vegetarian?" *Time/CNN*. 15 Jul 2002. Web. 1 Mar 2013. <http://web.archive.org/web/*/http://www.time.com/time/covers/1101020715/poll/>

Donovan, U. M., and R. S. Gibson. "Dietary Intakes of Adolescent Females Consuming Vegetarian, Semi-Vegetarian, and Omnivorous Diets." *Journal of Adolescent Health* 18 (1996):292–300.

"Download." *Food and Agriculture Organization of the United Nations FAOSTAT*. 2013. 1 Mar 2013. <http://faostat3.fao.org/home/index.html#DOWNLOAD>

Drewnowski, A., and S. E. Specter. "Poverty and Obesity: The Role of Energy Density and Energy Costs." *The American Journal of Clinical Nutrition* 79 (2004):6–16.

Eddy, T., Gallup, G., Jr., and D. Povinelli. "Attribution of Cognitive States of Animals: Anthropomorphism in Comparative Perspective." *Journal of Social Issues,* 49.1 (1993):87–101.

Einwohner, R. L. "Bringing the Outsiders In: Opponents' Claims and the Construction of Animal Rights Activists' Identity." *Mobilization: An International Journal* 7.3 (2002):253–268.

——. "Motivational Framing and Efficacy Maintenance: Animal Rights Activists' Use of Four Fortifying Strategies." *The Sociological Quarterly* 43.4 (2002):509–526.

Elzerman, J. E., Hoek, A. C., van Boekel, M. A. J. S., and P. A. Luning. "Consumer

Acceptance and Appropriateness of Meat Substitutes in a Meal Context." *Food Quality and Preference* 22 (2011):233–240.

Emerson, R. "Women Use Social Media More Than Men: Study." *The Huffington Post.* 26 Sep 2011. Web. 1 Mar 2013. <http://www.huffingtonpost.com/2011/09/23/women-use-social-media-more_n_978498.html>

"Farm Animal Welfare." *Humane Society of the United States.* 17 Nov 2011. 1 Mar 2013. <http://www.humanesociety.org/news/publications/whitepapers/farm_animal_welfare.html>

Feiler, D. C., Tost, L. P., and A. M. Grant. "Mixed Reasons, Missed Givings: The Costs of Blending Egoistic and Altruistic Reasons in Donation Requests." *Journal of Experimental Social Psychology* 48 (2012):1322–1328.

Fessler, M. T., Arguello, A. P., Mekdara, J. M., and R. Macias. "Disgust Sensitivity and Meat Consumption: A Test of an Emotivist Account of Moral Vegetarianism." *Appetite* 41 (2003):31–41.

Filippi, M., Riccitelli, G., Falini, A., Di Salle, F., Vuilleumier, P., Comi, G., and M. A. Rocca. "The Brain Functional Networks Associated to Human and Animal Suffering Differ among Omnivores, Vegetarians and Vegans." *PLoS ONE* 5.5 (2010):1–9.

"'Flexitarians' Driving Global Move Away From Meat Consumption: Study." *The Independent.* 31 Aug 2011. 1 Mar 2013. <http://www.independent.co.uk/life-style/flexitarians-driving-global-move-away-from-meat-consumption-study-2346860.html>

"Focus Groups for the Johns Hopkins Pilot Intervention of the Meatless Monday Campaign." *Humane Research Council.* 2007. 1 Mar 2013. <http://www.humanespot.org/content/focus-groups-johns-hopkins-pilot-intervention-meatless-monday-campaign>

Food and Nutrition Board, National Research Council. *What Is America Eating?: Proceedings of a Symposium.* FNB NRC, 1986. Web. 1 Mar 2013. <http://www.nap.edu/catalog.php?record_id=617>

Forestell, C. A., Spaeth, A. M., and S. A. Kane. "To Eat Or Not To Eat Red Meat. A Closer Look at the Relationship Between Restrained Eating and Vegetarianism in College Females." *Appetite* 58 (2012):319–325.

Fowler, R. Untitled Dissertation. Diss. Rutgers University, 2004. PDF file.

Fox, N., and K. J. Ward. "You Are What You Eat? Vegetarianism, Health and Identity." *Social Science & Medicine* 66 (2008):2585–2595.

Fox, N., and K. Ward. "Health, Ethics and Environment: A Qualitative Study of Vegetarian Motivations." *Appetite* 50 (2008):422–429.

Freeland-Graves, J. H., Greninger, S. A., and R. K. Young. "A Demographic and Social Profile of Age- and Sex-Matched Vegetarians and Nonvegetarians." *Journal of the American Dietetic Association* 86.7 (1986):907–913.

Freeland-Graves, J. H., Greninger, S. A., Graves, G. R., and R. K. Young. "Health Practices, Attitudes and Beliefs of Vegetarians and Non-Vegetarians." *Journal of the American Dietetic Association* 86.7 (1986):913–918.

Freeman, C. P. "Framing Animal Rights in the 'Go Veg' Campaigns of U.S. Animal Rights Organizations." *Society and Animals* 18 (2010):163–182.

———. "Meat's Place on the Campaign Menu: How U.S. Environmental Discourse Negotiates Vegetarianism." *Environmental Communication: A Journal of Nature and Culture* 4.3 (2010):255–276.

Gale, C. R., Deary, I. J., Schoon, I., and G. D. Batty. "IQ in Childhood and Vegetarianism in Adulthood: 1970 British Cohort Study." *British Medical Journal* 334 (2007).

Gallet, C. A. "The Income Elasticity of Meat: A Meta-Analysis." *The Australian Journal of Agricultural and Resource Economics* 54 (2010):477–490.

Galvin, S. L., and H. A. Herzog, Jr. "Attitudes and Dispositional Optimism of Animal Rights Demonstrators." *Society and Animals* 6.1 (1998):1–11.

———. "Ethical Ideology, Animal Rights Activism, and Attitudes Toward the Treatment of Animals." *Ethics & Behavior* 2.3 (1992):141–149.

Gilbody, S. M., Kirk, S. F. L., and A. J. Hill. "Vegetarianism in Young Women: Another Means of Weight Control?" *International Journal of Eating Disorders* 26 (1999):87–90.

"Giving USA 2012: The Annual Report on Philanthropy for the Year 2011." *The Giving Institute*. 2012. PDF file.

Glasser, C. L. "Simplifying Advocacy Materials—Understanding Decision Fatigue."

Humane Research Council. 21 Feb 2012. 1 Mar 2013. <http://www.humanespot .org/content/simplifying-advocacy-materials-understanding-decision-fatigue>

"Good News For Veggies: Personal Values Deceive Taste Buds." *Science Daily.* 18 Jul 2008. 1 Mar 2013. <http://www.sciencedaily.com/releases/2008/07/ 080716205208.htm>

Gossard, M. H., and R. York. "Social Structural Influences on Meat Consumption." *Research in Human Ecology* 10.1 (2003):1–9.

Goudreau, J. "What Men and Women Are Doing on Facebook." *Forbes.* 26 Apr 2010. Web. 1 Mar 2013. <http://www.forbes.com/2010/04/26/popular-social -networking-sites-forbes-woman-time-facebook-twitter_print.html>

Greene-Finestone, L. S., Campbell, M. K., Evers, S. E., and I. A. Gutamis. "Attitudes and Health Behaviors of Young Adolescent Omnivores and Vegetarians: A School-Based Study." *Appetite* 51 (2008):104–110.

Greenebaum, J. "Veganism, Identity and the Quest for Authenticity." *Food, Culture & Society* 15.1 (2012):129–144.

Grupe, B. "VO Feedback." E-mail to the author. 10 Jan 2013.

Gunert, K. G. "Future Trends and Consumer Lifestyles with Regard to Meat Consumption." *Meat Science* 74 (2006):149–160.

Gunther, A. "An Inquiry Into Animal Rights Vegan Activists' Perception and Practice of Persuasion." Diss. Simon Fraser University, 2012. Web. 1 Mar 2013.

Haddad, E. H., and J. S. Tanzman. "What Do Vegetarians in the United States Eat?" *The American Journal of Clinical Nutrition* 78 (Suppl) (2003):626S–632S.

Hamilton, M. "Disgust Reactions to Meat Among Ethically and Health Motivated Vegetarians." *Ecology of Food and Nutrition* 45 (2006):125–158.

——. "Eating Ethically: 'Spiritual' and 'Quasi-religious' Aspects of Vegetarianism." *Journal of Contemporary Religion* 15.1 (2000):65–83.

Hamilton, Malcolm. "Eating Death: Vegetarians, Meat and Violence." *Food, Culture & Society* 9.2 (2006):155–177.

Harrison, M. A. "Anthropomorphism, Empathy, and Perceived Communicative Ability Vary with Phylogenetic Relatedness to Humans." *Journal of Social, Evolutionary, and Cultural Psychology* 4.1 (2010):34–48.

Hartman Group. *Clicks & Cravings.* HG, 2012. PDF file. Web. <http://www.hartman -group.com/pdf/clicks-and-cravings-report-overview-and-order-form-2012 .pdf>

Haverstock, K., and D. K. Forgays. "To Eat or Not To Eat. A Comparison of Current and Former Animal Product Limiters." *Appetite* 58 (2012):1030–1036.

Havlicek, J., and P. Lenochova. "The Effect of Meat Consumption on Body Odor Attractiveness." *Chemical Senses* 31 (2006):747–752.

He, S., Fletcher, S., and A. Rimal. "Identifying Factors Influencing Beef, Poultry, and Seafood Consumption." *Journal of Food Distribution Research* 34.1 (2003):50–55.

Hecht, J. "Returning to Meat: Who Is Doing It, How It Happens, and What This Means for the Veg'n Movement." *Humane Research Council.* 2011. 1 Mar 2013. <http://www.humanespot.org/content/recidivism>

———. "Veg'n Recidivism: Why Is It Happening?" *Humane Research Council.* 2011. 1 Mar 2013. <http://spot.humaneresearch.org/content/veg%E2%80%99n-recidi-vism-why-it-happening>

———. "Where to Go From Here: Thoughts on Preventing Veg'n Recidivism." *Humane Research Council.* 2011. 1 Mar 2013. <http://www.humanespot.org/content/ where-go-here-thoughts-preventing-vegn-recidivism>

Heller, L. "Falling Soy Sales Call for Awareness Efforts, Mintel." *Food Navigator USA.* 13 Nov 2007. 1 Mar 2013 <http://www.foodnavigator-usa.com/Business/ Falling-soy-sales-call-for-awareness-efforts-Mintel>

Herzog, H. "Why Do Most Vegetarians Go Back to Eating Meat?" *Psychology Today.* 2011. 1 Mar 2013. <http://www.psychologytoday.com/blog/animals-and-us/ 201106/why-do-most-vegetarians-go-back-eating-meat>

Herzog, H. A. "Gender Differences in Human-Animal Interactions: A Review." *Anthrozoös* 20.1 (2007):7–21.

Herzog, H. A., and L. L. Golden. "Moral Emotions and Social Activism: The Case of Animal Rights." *Journal of Social Issues* 65.3 (2009):485–498.

Herzog, H. A., Jr., Betchart, N. S., and R. B. Pittman. "Gender, Sex Role Orientation, and Attitudes Toward Animals." *Anthrozoös* 4.3 (1991):184–191.

Herzog, H. A., Jr., "'The Movement Is My Life': The Psychology of Animal Rights Activism." *Journal of Social Issues* 49.1 (1993):103–119.

Hinze, A., Karg, C., van Zyl, M., Mohamed, N., and N. P. Steyn. "The Acceptability of Different Types of Soymilks Available in Cape Town in Consumers from High and Low Socio-Economic Areas." *International Journal of Consumer Studies* 28.1 (2004):40–48.

Hirschler, C. "'What Pushed Me Over the Edge was a Deer Hunter': Being Vegan in North America." *Society & Animals* 19 (2011):156–174.

Hirschler, C. A. "An Examination of Vegan's Beliefs and Experiences Using Critical Theory and Autoethnography." Diss. Cleveland State University, 2008. Web. 1 Mar 2013.

Hoek, A. C. "Will Novel Protein Foods Beat Meat? Consumer Acceptance of Meat Substitutes—A Multidisciplinary Research Approach?" Diss. Wageningen University, 2010. Web. 1 Mar 2013.

Hoek, A. C., Luning, P. A., Stafleu, A., and C. De Graaf. "Food-Related Lifestyle and Health Attitudes of Dutch Vegetarians, Non-Vegetarian Consumers of Meat Substitutes, and Meat Consumers." *Appetite* 42 (2004):265–272.

Hoek, A. C., Luning, P. A., Weijzen, P., Wengles, W., Kok, F. J., and C. de Graaf. "Replacement of Meat by Meat Substitutes. A Survey on Person- and Product-Related Factors in Consumer Acceptance." *Appetite* 56 (2011):662–673.

Hoek, A. C., van Boekel, M. A. J. S., Voordouw, J., and P. A. Luning. "Identification of New Food Alternatives: How Do Consumers Categorize Meat and Meat Substitutes?" *Food Quality and Preference* 22 (2011):371–383.

Hoffman, S. R., Stallings, S. F., Bessinger, R. C., and G. T. Brooks. "Differences Between Health and Ethical Vegetarians. Strength of Conviction, Nutrition Knowledge, Dietary Restriction, and Duration of Adherence." *Appetite*, in press. Epub ahead of print retrieved 4 Mar 2013. <http://www.sciencedirect.com/science/article/pii/S0195666313000676>

Holm, L., and M. Mohl. "The Role of Meat in Everyday Food Culture: An Analysis of an Interview Study in Copenhagen." *Appetite* 34 (2000):277–283.

Hoogland, C. T., de Boer, J., and J. J. Boersema. "Transparency of the Meat Chain in the Light of Food Culture and History." *Appetite* 45 (2005):15–23.

Hopkins, P. D., and A. Dacey. "Vegetarian Meat: Could Technology Save Animals and Satisfy Meat Eaters?" *Journal of Agricultural and Environmental Ethics* 21 (2008):579–596.

Horberg, E. J., Oveis, C., Keltner, D., and A. B. Cohen. "Disgust and the Moralization of Purity." *Journal of Personality and Social Psychology* 97.6 (2009): 963–976.

Horgen, K. B., and K. D. Brownell. "Comparison of Price Change and Health Message Interventions in Promoting Healthy Food Choices." *Health Psychology* 21.5 (2002):505–512.

Hormes, J. M., Fincher, K., Rozin, P., and M. C. Green. "Attitude Change After Reading a Book." N.d. TS.

Horowitz, R. *Putting Meat on the American Table: Taste, Technology, Transformation.* Baltimore: Johns Hopkins University Press, 2006.

"How Many Adults Are Vegan in the U.S.?" *Vegetarian Resource Group.* 5 Dec 2011. 1 Mar 2013. <http://www.vrg.org/blog/2011/12/05/how-many-adults-are-vegan - in-the-u-s/>

"How Many People Order Vegetarian Meals When Eating Out?" *Vegetarian Journal* 3 (2008):22–23.

"How Many Vegetarians Are There?" *Vegetarian Journal* 1 (2003). Web. 1 Mar 2013. <http://www.vrg.org/journal/vj2003issue3/vj2003issue3poll.htm>

"How Many Vegetarians Are There?" *Vegetarian Resource Group.* 15 May 2009. 1 Mar 2013. <http://www.vrg.org/press/2009poll.htm>

"How Many Vegetarians Are There?" *Vegetarian Resource Group.* 2000. 1 Mar 2013. <http://www.vrg.org/nutshell/poll2000.htm>

"How Often Do Americans Eat Vegetarian Meals? And How Many Adults in the U.S. Are Vegetarian?" *Vegetarian Resource Group.* 28 May 2012. 1 Mar 2013. <http:// www.vrg.org/blog/2012/05/18/how-often-do-americans-eat-vegetarian-meals -and-how-many-adults-in-the-u-s-are-vegetarian/>

Humane Research Council. *Advocating Meat Reduction and Vegetarianism to Adults in the U.S.* Humane Research Council, 2007. PDF file.

——. *Appendix: Phase One Survey Data (Total Sample Only).* Humane Research Council, 2007. PDF file.

——. *Focus Groups on Vegetarianism.* Humane Research Council, 2002. PDF file.

——. *How Many Vegetarians Are There?* Humane Research Council, 2010. PDF file.

———. *Results from MFA Survey of Females Age 13–35.* Humane Research Council, 2013. PDF file.

———. *Vegetarianism in the U.S.* Humane Research Council, 2005. PDF file.

———. *Why or Why Not Vegetarian.* Humane Research Council, 2008. PDF file.

Hung, I. W., and R. S. Wyer, Jr. "Differences in Perspective and the Influence of Charitable Appeals: When Imagining Oneself as the Victim Is Not Beneficial." *Journal of Marketing Research* 46 (2009):421–434.

Hussar, K. M., and P. L. Harris. "Children Who Choose Not to Eat Meat: A Study of Early Moral Decision-Making." *Social Development* 19.3 (2010):627–641.

"Industry Sales Figures." *Vegetarian Society of the UK.* 2012. 1 Mar 2013. <http://www.vegsoc.org/page.aspx?pid=754>

Ingenbleek, P. T. M., and V. M. Immink. "Consumer Decision-Making for Animal-Friendly Products: Synthesis and Implications." *Animal Welfare* 20 (2011):11–19.

Izmirli, S., and C. J. C. Phillips. "The Relationship Between Student Consumption of Animal Products and Attitudes to Animals in Europe and Asia." *British Food Journal* 113.3 (2011):436–450.

Jabs, J., Devine, C. M., and J. Sobal. "Model of the Process of Adopting Vegetarian Diets: Health Vegetarians and Ethical Vegetarians." *Journal for Nutrition Education* 30.4 (1998):196–202.

Jabs, J., Sobal, J., and C. M. Devine. "Managing Vegetarianism: Identities, Norms and Interactions." *Ecology of Food and Nutrition* 39 (2000):375–394.

Jamieson, A. "Don't Call It Vegetarian, It Is 'Meat-Free.'" *Telegraph.* 16 Jan 2011. Web. 1 Mar 2013. <http://www.telegraph.co.uk/finance/newsbysector/retailandconsumer/8261614/Dont-call-it-vegetarian-it-is-meat-free.html>

Janda, S. and P. J. Trocchia. "Vegetarianism: Toward A Greater Understanding." *Psychology & Marketing* 18.12 (2001):1205–1240.

Jasper, J. M., and J. D. Poulsen. "Recruiting Strangers and Friends: Moral Shocks and Social Networks in Animal Rights and Anti-Nuclear Protests." *Social Problems* 42.4 (1995):493–512.

Jeltsen, M. "Vegetarianism, Eating Disorder Study Reveals Worrisome Relation-

ship Among Women." *Huffington Post.* 2 Aug 2012. 1 Mar 2013. <http://www
.huffingtonpost.com/2012/08/01/vegetarianism-eating-disorders-more
-likely_n_1729326.html>

Jones, D. M. "Advertising Animal Protection." *Anthrozoös* 10.4 (1997):151–159.

Judge, M. "Attitudes Toward People Based on Their Dietary Identity." *Humane Research Council.* 18 Sep 2012. 1 Mar 2013. <http://www.humanespot.org/content/
social-and-ideological-foundations-meat-consumption-and-vegetarianism>

——. "The Social and Ideological Foundations of Meat Consumption and Vegetarianism." *Humane Research Council.* 4 Sep 2012. 1 Mar 2013. <http://www
.humanespot.org/content/social-and-ideological-foundations-meat
-consumption-and-vegetarianism>

Kahkonen. P., and H. Tuorila. "Effect of Reduced-Fat Information on Expected and Actual Hedonic and Sensory Ratings of Sausage." *Appetite* 30.1 (1998):13–23.

Kalof, L., Dietz, T., Stern, P. C., and G. A. Guagnano. "Social Psychological and Structural Influences on Vegetarian Beliefs." *Rural Sociology* 64.3 (1999):500–511.

Kelly, C. W. "Commitment to Health: A Predictor of Dietary Change." *Journal of Clinical Nursing* 20 (2011):2830–2836.

Kenyon, P. E., and M. E. Barker. "Attitudes Toward Meat-Eating in Vegetarian and Non-Vegetarian Teenage Girls in England—an Ethnographic Approach." *Appetite* 30 (1998):185–198.

Ketchum. *Food 2020: The Consumer as CEO.* Ketchum, 2008. PDF file.

Key, T. J., Fraser, G. E., Thorogood, M., Appleby, P. N., Beral, V., Reeves, G., Burr, M. L., Chang-Claude, J., Frentzel-Beyme, R., Kuzma, J. W., Mann, J., and K. McPherson. "Mortality in Vegetarians and Nonvegetarians: Detailed Findings from a Collaborative Analysis of 5 Prospective Studies." *The American Journal of Clinical Nutrition* 70 (Suppl) (1999):516S–524S.

Kim, E. H., Schroeder, K. M., Houser, Jr., R. F., and J. T. Dwyer. "Two Small Surveys, 25 Years Apart, Investigation Motivations of Dietary Choice in 2 Groups of Vegetarians in the Boston Area." *Journal of the American Dietetic Association* 99.5 (1999):598–601.

"Kings of the Carnivores." *The Economist.* 30 Apr 2012. Web. 1 Mar 2013. <http://
www.economist.com/blogs/graphicdetail/2012/04/daily-chart-17>

Knight, S. E., Vrij, A., Cherryman, J., & K. Nunkoosing. "Attitudes Toward Animal Use and Belief in Animal Mind." *Anthrozoös* 17 (2004):43–62.

Knight, S., and H. Herzog. "All Creatures Great and Small: New Perspectives on Psychology and Human–Animal Interactions." *Journal of Social Issues* 65.3 (2009):451–461.

Knight, S., Bard, K., Vrij, A., and D. Brandon. "Human Rights, Animal Wrongs? Exploring Attitudes Toward Animal Use and Possibilities for Change." *Society and Animals* 18 (2010):251–272.

Knight, S., Vrij, A., Cherryman, J., and K. Nunkoosing. "Attitudes Toward Animal Use and Belief in Animal Mind." *Anthrozoös* 17.1 (2004):43–62.

Krizmanic, J. "Here's Who We Are." *Vegetarian Times* Oct 1992:72–80. Print.

Kruse, C. R. "Gender, Views of Nature, and Support for Animal Rights." *Society and Animals* 7.3 (1999):179–198.

Kubberod, E. "Not Just a Matter of Taste—Disgust in the Food Domain." Diss. B I Norwegian School of Management, 2005. Web. 1 Mar 2013.

Kubberod, E., Ueland, O., Dingstad, G. I., Risvik, E., and I. J. Henjesand. "The Effect of Animality in the Consumption Experience—A Potential for Disgust." *Journal of Food Products Marketing* 14 (2008):103–124.

Kubberod, E., Ueland, O., Rodbotten, M., Westad, F., and E. Risvik. "Gender Specific Preferences and Attitudes Toward Meat." *Food Quality and Preference* 13 (2002):285–294.

Larsson, C. L., Klock, K. S., Astrom, A. N., Haugejorden, O., and G. Johansson. "Lifestyle-related Characteristics of Young Low-Meat Consumers and Omnivores in Sweden and Norway." *Journal of Adolescent Health* 21 (2002):190–198.

Latvala, T., Niva, M., Makela, J., Pouta, E., Heikkila, J., Koistinen, L., Forsman-Hugg, S., and J. Kotro. "Meat Consumption Patterns and Intentions for Change Among Finnish Consumers." *EAAE 2011 Congress on Change and Uncertainty*. Zurich: ETH Zurich, 2011.

Latvala, T., Niva, M., Makela, J., Pouta, E., Heikkila, J., Kotro, J., and S. Forsman-Hugg. "Diversifying Meat Consumption Patterns: Consumers' Self-Reported Past Behavior and Intentions for Change." *Meat Science* 92 (2012):71–77.

Lawrence, V. "Is Vegetarianism a Diet or an Ideology." *Canadian Medical Association Journal* 148.6 (1993):998–1002.

Lea, E. J. "Moving from Meat: Vegetarianism, Beliefs and Information Sources." Diss. The University of Adelaide, 2001. Web. 1 Mar 2013.

Lea, E. J., Crawford, D., and A. Worsley. "Consumers' Readiness to Eat a Plant-Based Diet." *European Journal of Clinical Nutrition* 60 (2006):342–351.

——. "Public Views of the Benefits and Barriers to the Consumption of a Plant-Based Diet." *European Journal of Clinical Nutrition* 60 (2006):828–837.

Lea, E. and A. Worsley. "Benefits and Barriers to the Consumption of a Vegetarian Diet in Australia." *Public Health Nutrition* 6.5 (2002):505–511.

——. "The Factors Associated with the Belief that Vegetarian Diets Provide Health Benefits." *Asia Pacific Journal of Clinical Nutrition* 12.3 (2003):296–303.

——. "Influences on Meat Consumption in Australia." *Appetite* 36 (2001):127–136.

Lewis, J. E. "Dream Reports of Animal Rights Activists." *Dreaming* 18.3 (2008):181–200.

Lin, B., Yen, S., and C. Davis. "Consumer Knowledge and Meat Consumption in the U.S." *Gold Coast*. 2006. Web. 1 Mar 2013. <http://ageconsearch.umn.edu/bitstream/25258/1/pp060674.pdf>

Lindeman, M. "The State of Mind of Vegetarians: Psychological Well-Being or Distress?" *Ecology of Food and Nutrition* 41 (2002):75–86.

Lindeman, M., and K. Stark. "Pleasure, Pursuit of Health or Negotiation of Identity? Personality Correlates of Food Choice Motives Among Young and Middle-Aged Women." *Appetite* 33 (1999):141–161.

Lindeman, M., Stark, K., and K. Latvala. "Vegetarianism and Eating-Disordered Thinking." *Eating Disorders* 8 (2000):157–165.

"Lisa the Vegetarian." Wikipedia. 2013. 1 Mar 2013. <http://www.en.wikipedia.org/wiki/Lisa_the_Vegetarian>

"Looking for Foods That Are Good for Both You and the Environment?" *Reuters*. 3 Jan 2008. Web. 1 Mar 2013. <http://www.reuters.com/article/2008/01/02/idUS110255+02-Jan-2008+PRN20080102>

Loughnan, S., Haslam, N., and B. Bastian. "The Role of Meat Consumption in the Denial of Moral Status and Mind to Meat Animals." *Appetite* 55 (2010):156–159.

Lusk, J. L., and F. B. Norwood. "Some Economic Benefits and Costs of Vegetarianism." *Agricultural and Resource Economics Review* 38.2 (2009):109–124.

"Mac vs. PC: A Hunch Rematch." *Hunch.* 21 Apr 2011. 1 Mar 2013. <http://blog
.hunch.com/?p=45344>

MacNair, R. M. "McDonald's 'Empirical Look at Becoming Vegan'." *Society & Animals*
9.1 (2001):63–69.

———. "The Psychology of Becoming a Vegetarian." *Vegetarian Nutrition: An International Journal* 2.3 (1998):96–102.

"Maintaining Vegetarian Diets: Personal Factors, Social Networks, and Environmental Resources." *Humane Research Council*, 2008. <http://www.humanespot.
org/content/maintaining-vegetarian-diets-personal-factors-social-networks-and
-environmental-resources>

Martins, Y., Pliner, P., and R. O'Connor. "Restrained Eating Among Vegetarians: Does A
Vegetarian Lifestyle Mask Concerns About Weight?" *Appetite* 32 (1999):145–154.

Massimo, F., Riccitelli, G., Meani, A., Falini, A., Comi, G., and M. A. Rocca. "The 'Vegetarian Brain': Chatting with Monkeys and Pigs." *Brain Structure and Function* (Sep
2012).

Matheny, G. "Expected Utility, Contributory Causation, and Vegetarianism." *Journal
of Applied Philosophy* 19.3 (2002):293–297.

Mathews, S., and H. A. Herzog, Jr. "Personality and Attitudes Toward the Treatment
of Animals." *Society and Animals* 5.2 (1997):169–175.

Maurer, D. *Vegetarianism: Movement or Moment?* Philadelphia: Temple University
Press, 2002.

McCarty, R. "Who Are Socially Conscious Consumers … and How Do We Talk to Them?"
Beef Issues Quarterly. 17 Aug 2012. 1 Mar 2013. <http://www.beefissuesquarterly.com/
whoaresociallyconsciousconsumersandhowdowetalktothem.aspx>

McDonald, B. "'Once You Know Something, You Can't Not Know It': An Empirical
Look at Becoming Vegan." Society & Animals 8 (2000):1–23.

McEachern, M. G. "Consumer Perceptions of Meat Production." *British Food Journal*
107.8 (2005):572–593.

McGrath, E. "The Politics of Veganism." *Social Alternatives* 19.4 (2000):50–59

McIlveen, H., Abraham, C., and G. Armstrong. "Meat Avoidance and the Role of Re-
placers." *Nutrition & Food Science* 1 (1999):29–36.

McPherson, K. D. "What About Fish? Why Some 'Vegetarians' Eat Seafood and Implications for the Vegetarian Movement?" Diss. Tufts University, 2012. *Microsoft Word* file.

"Meat Consumption Among Whites, Hispanics, and African Americans in the U.S." *Humane Research Council.* 2007. 1 Mar 2013. <www.humanespot.org/content/meat-consumption-among-whites-hispanics-and-african-americans-us>

"Meat Consumption Per Person, KG, 2007." *Scribd.* 2012. 1 Mar 2013. <http://www.scribd.com/doc/91840616/Meat-Consumption-Per-Person>

Mela D. J. "Food Choice and Intake: The Human Factor." Proceedings of the Nutrition Society 58.3 (1999):513–21.

Merriman, B. "Gender Differences in Family and Peer Reaction to the Adoption of a Vegetarian Diet." *Feminism & Psychology* 20.3 (2010):420–427.

Michalak, J., Zhang, X. C., and F. Jacobi. "Vegetarian Diet and Mental Disorders: Results from a Representative Community Survey." *International Journal of Behavioral Nutrition and Physical Activity* 9 (2012):67.

Minson, J. A., and B. Monin. "Do-Gooder Derogation: Disparaging Morally Motivated Minorities to Defuse Anticipated Reproach." *Social Psychological and Personality Science* 3.2 (2012):200–207.

Montero, C. *Untitled Document.* PDF file, 2012.

Mooney, K. M., and L. Walbourn. "When College Students Reject Food: Not Just a Matter of Taste." *Appetite* 36 (2001):41–50.

Moore, D. W. "Public Lukewarm on Animal Rights." *Gallup.* 21 May 2003. Web. 1 Mar 2013. <http://www.gallup.com/poll/8461/public-lukewarm-animal-rights.aspx>

Morris, M. C. "Improved Animal Welfare Is More Related to Inequality Than It Is to Income." 2012. *Microsoft Word* file.

Muhammad, A., Seale, Jr., J. L., Meade, B., and A. Regmi. *International Evidence on Food Consumption Patterns: An Update Using 2005 International Comparison Program Data.* TB-1929. U.S. Dept. of Agriculture, Econ. Res. Serv. March 2011.

Muirhead, S. "Survey: Why Some Choose Not to Eat Meat." *Feedstuffs FoodLink.* 2011. 1 Mar 2013 <http://feedstuffsfoodlink.com/story-survey-why-some-choose-not-to-eat-meat-0-66580>

Muise, A., Impett, E. A., Kogan, A., and S. Desmarais. "Keeping the Spark Alive: Being Motivated to Meet a Partner's Sexual Needs Sustains Sexual Desire in Long-Term Romantic Relationships." *Social Psychological and Personality Science.* In press.

Munro, L. "Caring About Blood, Flesh, and Pain: Women's Standing in the Animal Protection Movement." *Society & Animals* 9.1 (2001):43–61.

Murcott, A. "Social Influences on Food Choice and Dietary Change: A Sociological Attitude." *Proceedings of the Nutrition Society* 54 (1995):729–735.

Murtaugh, M. A., Ma, K., Sweeney, C., Caan, B. J., and M. L. Slattery. "Meat Consumption Patterns and Preparation, Genetic Variants of Metabolic Enzymes, and Their Association with Rectal Cancer in Men and Women." *The Journal of Nutrition* 134 (2004):776–784.

Nath, J. "Gendered Fare? A Qualitative Investigation of Alternative Food and Masculinities." *Journal of Sociology* 47.3 (2011):261–278.

"National Health and Nutrition Examination Survey." *Centers for Disease Control and Prevention.* 2011. 1 Mar 2013. <http://www.cdc.gov/nchs/nhanes/nhanes2009-2010/nhanes09_10.htm>

Netburn, D. "Research Shows Women More Active on Facebook Than Men." *Los Angeles Times.* 3 Feb 2012. Web. 1 Mar 2013. <http://www.standard.net/stories/2012/02/03/research-shows-women-more-active-facebook-men>

"New Research Shows Consumers Streaming to Internet." *The Center for Food Integrity.* 6 Oct 2010. 1 Mar 2013. <http://www.foodintegrity.org/document_center/download/News_section/2010ResearchRelease.pdf>

Newport, F. "In U.S., 5% Consider Themselves Vegetarians." *Gallup.* 26 Jul 2012. 1 Mar 2013. <http://www.gallup.com/poll/156215/Consider-Themselves-Vegetarians.aspx>

——. "Post-Derby Tragedy, 38% Support Banning Animal Racing." Gallup. 15 May 2008. Web. 1 Mar 2013. <http://www.gallup.com/poll/107293/postderby-tragedy-38-support-banning-animal-racing.aspx>

Nierenberg, D. and L. Reynolds. "Disease and Drought Curb Meat Production and Consumption." *WorldWatch Institute.* 23 Oct 2012. 1 Mar 2013. <http://www.worldwatch.org/disease-and-drought-curb-meat-production-and-consumption-0>

Nobis, N. "The 'Babe' Vegetarians: Bioethics, Animal Minds and Moral Methodology." 2012. PDF file.

Norwood, F. B., and J. L. Lusk. *Compassion, by the Pound: The Economics of Farm Animal Welfare.* New York: Oxford University Press, 2011.

"Number of Calories Killed to Produce One Million Calories in Eight Food Categories." *Animal Visuals.* 12 Oct 2009. 1 Mar 2013. <http://www.animalvisuals.org/projects/data/1mc>

"Number of UK Vegetarians." *Vegetarian Society of the UK.* 2012. 1 Mar 2013. <http://www.vegsoc.org/page.aspx?pid=753>

"Obesity (Most Recent) By Country." *NationMaster.* 2005. 1 Mar 2013. <http://www.nationmaster.com/red/graph/hea_obe-health-obesity&b_printable=1>

Ogden, J., Karim, L., Choudry, A., and K. Brown. "Understanding Successful Behaviour Change: The Role of Intentions, Attitudes to the Target and Motivations and the Example of Diet." *Health Education Research* 22.3 (2007):397–405.

Ornish, N. "Eat More, Weigh Less: Dr. Dean Ornish's Life Choice Program for Losing Weight Safely While Eating Abundantly." New York: HarperCollins, 2001.

Paisley, J., Beanlands, H., Goldman, J., Evers, S., and J. Chappell. "Dietary Change: What Are the Responses and Roles of Significant Others?" *Journal of Nutrition Education and Behavior* 40.2 (2008):80–88.

Partridge, S. A., and P. R. Amato. "Vegetarian Sex." *EatVeg.* 2006. 1 Mar 2013. <http://www.eatveg.com/vegansex.htm>

Paul, E. S., and J. A. Serpell. "Childhood Pet Keeping and Humane Attitudes in Young Adulthood." *Animal Welfare* 2 (1993):321–337.

"Per Capita Poultry Consumption Comparison With Other Animal Protein Sources." *Agriculture and Agri-Food Canada.* 2013. 1 Mar 2013. <http://www.agr.gc.ca/poultry/consm_eng.htm>

Perry, C. L., McGuire, M. T., Neumark-Sztainer, D., and M. Story. "Characteristics of Vegetarian Adolescents in a Multiethnic Urban Population." *Journal of Adolescent Health* 29.6 (2001):406-416.

Phillips, C., Izmirli, S., Aldavood, J., Alonso, M., Choe, B., Hanlon, A., Handziska, A., Illmann, G., Keeling, L., Kennedy, M., Lee, G., Lund, V., Mejdell, C., Pelagic, V., and T. Rehn. "An International Comparison of Female and Male Students' Attitudes to the Use of Animals." *Animals* 1 (2011):7–26.

Plous, S. "An Attitude Survey of Animal Rights Activists." *Psychological Science* 2.3 (1991):194–196.

——. "Signs of Change Within the Animal Rights Movement: Results From a Follow-Up Survey of Activists." *Journal of Comparative Psychology* 112.1 (1998):48–54.

"PMA Research Reveals Snapshot of Vegetarians, New Flexitarians." *Produce Marketing Association*. 2006. 1 Mar 2013. <http://www.freshplaza.com/2006/28sep/1-1_us_pma.htm>

Pollard, T. M., Steptoe, A., and J. Wardle. "Motives Underlying Healthy Eating: Using the Food Choice Questionnaire to Explain Variation in Dietary Intake." *Journal of Biosocial Science* 30 (1998):165–179.

Potts, A., and M. White. *Cruelty-Free Consumption in New Zealand*. New Zealand Centre for Human-Animal Studies, May 2007. PDF file.

Povey, R., Wellens, B., and M. Conner. "Attitudes Toward Following Meat, Vegetarian, and Vegan Diets: An Examination of the Role of Ambivalence." *Appetite* 37 (2001):15–26.

Powell, K. A. "Lifestyle as Rhetorical Transaction: A Case Study of the Vegetarian Movement in the United States." *Atlantic Journal of Communication* 10.2 (2002):169–190.

Powell, K. D. "Lifestyle as a Dimension of Social Movement Study: A Case Study of the Vegetarian Movement in the United States." Diss. University of Georgia, 1992. Web. 1 Mar. 2013.

Preylo, B. D., and H. Arikawa. "Comparison of Vegetarians and Non-Vegetarians on Pet Attitude and Empathy." *Anthrozoös* 21.4 (2008):387–395.

Pribis, P., Pencak, R. C., and T. Grajales. "Beliefs and Attitudes Toward Vegetarian Lifestyle Across Generations." *Nutrients* 2 (2010):523–531.

Priority Ventures Group. *Vegetarian Means Business*. Priority Ventures Group, 2011. PDF file.

"Public Attitudes/Consumer Behavior." *Vegetarian Society of the UK*. 2012. 1 Mar 2013. <http://www.vegsoc.org/page.aspx?pid=755>

Qammar, G., Mohy-ud-Din, G., Huma, N., Sameen, A., and M. I. Khan. "Textured Soy Protein (TSP) as Pizza Topping." *Nutrition & Food Science* 40.6 (2010):551–556.

Ranganath, K. A., Spellman, B. A., and J. A. Joy-Gaba. "Cognitive 'Category-Based Induction' Research and Social 'Persuasion' Research Are Each About What Makes Arguments Believable: A Tale of Two Literatures." *Perspectives on Psychological Science* 5.2 (2010):115–122.

Rao, D., Yarowsky, D., Shreevats, A., and M. Gupta. "Classifying Latent User Attributes in Twitter." *SMUC'10 Proceedings of the 2nd International Workshop on Search and Mining User-Generated Contents.* New York: Association for Computing Machinery, 2010. Web.

"Readability of Vegan Outreach Literature." *The Humane Research Council.* 2012. 1 Mar 2013. <http://www.humanespot.org/content/readability-vegan-outreach-literature>

"Report: Number of Animals Killed in US Increases in 2010." *Farm Animal Rights Movement.* 2011. 1 Mar 2013. <http://www.farmusa.org/statistics11.html>

"Research Adds Weight to Meat-Free Strategy." *Food Navigator.* 2007. 1 Mar 2013. <http://www.foodnavigator.com/Financial-Industry/Research-adds-weight-to-meat-free-strategy>

Richards, M. "Childhood Intelligence and Being a Vegetarian." *British Medical Journal* 334 (2007):216–217.

Richardson, N. J., Shepherd, R., and N. A. Elliman. "Current Attitudes and Future Influences on Meat Consumption in the U.K." *Appetite* 21 (1993):41–51.

Richardson, N. J., Shepherd, R., and N. Elliman. "Meat Consumption, Definition of Meat and Trust in Information Sources in the UK Population and Members of the Vegetarian Society." *Ecology of Food and Nutrition* 33 (1994):1–13.

Rimal, A. P. "Factors Affecting Meat Preferences Among American Consumers." *Family Economics and Nutrition Review.* 14.2 (2002):36–43.

Roberts, S. A., Dibble, S. L., Nussey, B., and K. Casey. "Cardiovascular Disease Risk in Lesbian Women." *Women's Health Issues* 13 (2003):167–174.

Roche, D. "The Role of Vegetarian Options in Campus Dining: Acceptability of Vegetarian Burgers." Diss. Eastern Illinois University, 2012. Web. 1 Mar 2013.

"Roper Poll on Reasons for Vegetarianism, 1989 [Not Actual Title]." *Humane Research*

Council. 2007. 1 Mar 2013. <http://www.humanespot.org/content/roper-poll
-reasons-vegetarianism-1989-not-actual-title#more2094>

Rosegrant, M. W., Paisner, M. S., Meijer, S., and J. Witcover. *Global Food Projections to
2020.* International Food Policy Research Institute, 2011. PDF file.

Rothberger, H. "Real Men Don't Eat (Vegetable) Quiche: Masculinity and the Justi-
fication of Meat Consumption." *Psychology of Men & Masculinity* (Nov 12, 2012).

Rousset, S., Deiss, V., Juillard, E., Schlich, P., and S. Droit-Volet. "Emotions Generated by Meat and Other Food Products in Women." *British Journal of Nutrition* 94
(2005):609–619.

Rozin, P., Bauer, R., and D. Catanese. "Food and Life, Pleasure and Worry, Among
American College Students: Gender Differences and Regional Similarities." *Journal of Personality and Social Psychology* 85.1 (2003):132–141.

Rozin, P., Hormes, J. M., Faith, M. S., and B. Wansink. "Is Meat Male? A Quantitative
Multimethod Framework to Establish Metaphoric Relationships." *Journal of Consumer Research* 39 (2012):629–643.

Rozin, P., Markwith, M., and C. Stoess. "Moralization and Becoming a Vegetarian:
The Transformation of Preferences Into Values and the Recruitment of Disgust."
Psychological Science 8.2 (1997):67–73.

Ruby, M. "Vegetarianism. A Blossoming Field of Study." *Appetite* 58 (2012):141–150.

Ruby, M. B., and S. J. Heine. "Meat, Morals and Masculinity." *Appetite* 56 (2011):447–450.

——. "Too Close to Home. Factors Predicting Meat Avoidance." *Appetite* 59
(2012):47–52.

Rudder, C. "10 Charts About Sex." *OK Cupid.* 19 Apr 2011. 1 Mar 2013. <http://www
.blog.okcupid.com/index.php/10-charts-about-sex/>

Ryan, C. L., and J. Siebens. *Education Attainment in the United States: 2009.* United
States Census Bureau, 2012. PDF File.

Sadler, M. "Meat Alternatives—Market Developments and Health Benefits." *Trends
in Food Science & Technology* 15 (2004):250–260.

Saja, K. "The Moral Footprint of Animal Products." *Agriculture and Human Values* (2012).

Sanday, P. *Female Power and Male Dominance: On the Origins of Sexual Inequality.* Cambridge: Cambridge University Press, 1981.

Santos, M. L. S., and D. A. Booth. "Influences on Meat Avoidance Among British Students." *Appetite* 27 (1996):197–205.

Schafer, C., Neidhart, S., and R. Carle. "Application and Sensory Evaluation of Enzymatically Texturised Vegetable Proteins in Food Models." *European Food Research and Technology* 232 (2011):1043–1056.

Schosler, H., de Boer, J., and J. Boersema. "Can We Cut Out the Meat of the Dish? Constructing Consumer-Oriented Pathways Toward Meat Substitution." *Appetite* 58 (2012):39–47.

Schroeter, C., and K. Foster. "The Impact of Health Information and Women in the Work Force on Aggregate Meat Demand." *Purdue Agricultural Economics Report,* Aug 2004. Web. 1 Mar 2013. <http://www.agecon.purdue.edu/extension/pubs/paer/2004/paer0804.pdf>

Sethu, H. "How Many Animals Does a Vegetarian Save?" *Counting Animals.* 6 Feb 2012. 1 Mar 2013. <http://www.countinganimals.com/how-many-animals-does-a-vegetarian-save/>

———. "Meat Consumption and Demand Both in Decline." *Counting Animals.* 20 Nov 2012. 1 Mar 2013. <http://countinganimals.com/meat-consumption-and-demand-both-in-decline/>

Sheeran, P. *Does Changing Attitudes, Norms or Self-Efficacy Change Intentions and Behaviour? End of Award Report.* Swindon: Economic and Social Research Council (2006). <http://www.esrc.ac.uk/my-esrc/grants/RES-000-22-0847/outputs/Download/95999bba-ea81-4537-b653-f2ba01493781>.

Shields, S. "Hey Sara!" E-mail to the author. 7 Feb 2013.

Shprintzen, A. D. "Looks Like Meat, Smells Like Meat, Tastes Like Meat: Battle Creek, Protose and the Making of Modern American Vegetarianism." *Food, Culture & Society* 15.1 (2012):113-128.

Signal, T. D., and N. Taylor. "Attitudes to Animals in the Animal Protection Community Compared to a Normative Community Sample." *Society & Animals* 14.3 (2006):265–274.

Smith, C. F., Burke, L. E., and R. R. Wing. "Vegetarian and Weight-Loss Diets Among Young Adults." *Obesity Research* 8.2 (2000):123–129.

Sobal, J. "Men, Meat, and Marriage: Models of Masculinity." *Food and Foodways:*

Explorations in the History and Culture of Human Nourishment 13 (2005):135–158.

Speedy, A. W. "Global Production and Consumption of Animal Source Foods." *The Journal of Nutrition* (Suppl) (2003):4048S–4053S.

Spencer, E. H., Elon, L. K., and E. Frank. "Personal and Professional Correlates of U.S. Medical Students' Vegetarianism." *Journal of the American Dietetic Association* 107 (2007):72–78.

Stahler, C. "How Many Adults Are Vegetarian." *Vegetarian Journal* 4 (2006). Web. 1 Mar 2013. <http://www.vrg.org/journal/vj2006issue4/vj2006issue4poll.htm 1/5>

———. "How Many Vegetarians Are There?" *Vegetarian Resource Group.* 1994. 1 Mar 2013. <http://www.vrg.org/nutshell/poll.htm>

———. "How Many Youth Are Vegetarian?" *The Vegetarian Research Group.* 2010. 1 Mar 2013. <http://www.vrg.org/press/youth_poll_2010.php>

———. "How Often Do Americans Eat Vegetarian Meals? And How Many Adults in the U.S. Are Vegan?" *The Vegetarian Resource Group.* 2011. 1 March 2013. <http://www.vrg.org/journal/vj2011issue4/vj2011issue4poll.php>.

———. "Retention Survey—2009." *Vegetarian Resource Group.* 2009. 1 Mar 2013. <http://www.vrg.org/research/retention_survey_2009.php>

———. "Sugar, Vegan Deli Slices, Whole Grains, Meat Genes—What Will Vegans and Vegetarians Eat? VRG Asks in a New National Harris Poll." *Vegetarian Resource Group.* 18 Apr 2012. 1 Mar 2013. <http://www.sciencedaily.com/releases/2008/07/080716205208.htm>

Stahler, C., and D. Wasserman. "Reader Survey Results." *Vegetarian Journal* 17.1 (1998). Web. 1 Mar 2013. <http://www.vrg.org/journal/vj98jan/981coord.htm>

"Statistics." *Vegetarian Society of the UK.* 2012. 1 Mar 2013. <http://www.vegsoc.org/page.aspx?pid=750>

Stein, R. I., and C. J. Nemeroff. "Moral Overtones of Food: Judgments of Others Based on What They Eat." *Food and Morality* 21.5 (1995):480–490.

Stiles, B. L. "Vegetarianism: Identity and Experiences as Factors in Food Selection." *Free Inquiry in Creative Sociology* 26.2 (1998):213–225.

Stubbs, J., Ferres, S, and G. Horgan. "Energy Density of Foods: Effects on Energy Intake." *Critical Reviews in Food Science and Nutrition* 40.6 (2000):481–515.

"Survey for National Vegetarian Week." *Humane Research Council.* 2010. 1 Mar 2013. <http://www.humanespot.org/content/survey-national-vegetarian-week>

Swanson, J. E., Rudman, L. A., and A. G. Greenwald. "Using the Implicit Association Test to Investigate Attitude-Behaviour Consistency for Stigmatised Behaviour." *Cognition and Emotion* 15.2 (2001):207–230.

Taylor, N., and T. D. Signal. "Empathy and Attitudes to Animals." *Anthrozoös* 18.1 (2005):18–27.

Templer, D. I., Connelly, H. J., Bassman, L., and J. Hart. "Construction and Validation of an Animal–Human Continuity Scale." *Social Behavior and Personality* 34.7 (2006):769–776.

The Center on Philanthropy at Indiana University. *Giving USA 2012.* CPIU, 2012. PDF file.

"The Humane League—HiddenFaceOfFood.com Facebook Ads Survey—Fall 2011." *The Humane League.* 2011. 1 Mar 2013. <http://www.thehumaneleague com/extra/FacebookAdsSurveyResults2011.pdf>

"The Modern Canadian Male: 96% Eat Meat, 98% Avoid Yoga." *Humane Research Council.* 2008. 1 Mar 2013. <http://www.humaneresearch.org/content/modern -canadian-male-96-eat-meat-98-avoid-yoga>

"The One (Really Easy) Persuasion Technique Everyone Should Know." *PsyBlog.* 7 Feb 2013. 1 Mar 2013. <http://www.spring.org.uk/2013/02/the-one-really -easy-persuasion-technique-everyone-should-know.php>

"The TRU Study." *Humane Research Council.* 2007. 1 Mar 2013. <http://www .humanespot.org/content/tru-study>

THL Ad Gender Comparisons. The Humane League, 2012. *Microsoft Excel* file.

"Time/CNN Poll on Vegetarianism [Not Actual Title]." *Humane Research Council.* 2007. 1 Mar 2013. <http://www.humanespot.org/content/timecnn-poll -vegetarianism-not-actual-title#more2247>

Timko, C. A., Hormes, J. M., and J. Chubski. "Will the Real Vegetarian Please Stand Up? An Investigation of Dietary Restraint and Eating Disorder Symptoms in Vegetarians Versus Non-Vegetarians." *Appetite* 58 (2012):982–990.

Tiplady, C. M., Walsh, D. B., and C. J. C. Phillips. "Public Response to Media Coverage of Animal Cruelty." *Journal of Agricultural and Environmental Ethics* (July 2012).

Tobler, C., Visschers, V., and M. Siegrist. "Eating Green. Consumers' Willingness to Adopt Ecological Food Consumption Behaviors." *Appetite* 57 (2011):674–682.

Tonsor, G., and N. Olynk. "Impacts of Animal Well-Being and Welfare Media on Meat Demand." *Journal of Agricultural Economics* 62 (2011):59–72.

Tu, V. P., Husson, F., Sutan, A., Ha, D. T., and D. Valentin. "For Me the Taste of Soy Is Not a Barrier to Its Consumption. And How About You?" *Appetite* 58 (2012):914–921.

Tukker, A., Emmert, S., Charter, M., Vezzoli, C., Svo, E., Andersen, M. M., Geerken, T., Tischner, U., and S. Lahlou. "Fostering Change to Sustainable Consumption and Production: An Evidence-Based View." *Journal of Cleaner Production* 16 (2008):1218–1225.

United States Census Bureau. *Educational Attainment in the United States: 2009.* Feb 2012. Web. 1 Mar 2013. <http://www.census.gov/prod/2012pubs/p20-566.pdf>

United States Department of Agriculture Economic Research Service. *Commodity Consumption by Population Characteristics.* 18 Sep 2012. Web. 1 Mar 2013. <http://www.ers.usda.gov/data-products/commodity-consumption-by-population-characteristics.aspx>

———. *Factors Affecting U.S. Beef Consumption.* Oct 2005. Web. 1 Mar 2013. <http://www.ers.usda.gov/media/864436/ldpm13502_002.pdf>

———. *Factors Affecting U.S. Pork Consumption.* May 2005. Web. 1 Mar 2013. <http://www.ers.usda.gov/media/326138/ldpm13001_1_.pdf>

———. "Livestock & Meat Domestic Data," 2013. <http://www.ers.usda.gov/data-products/livestock-meat-domestic-data.aspx>

United States Department of Agriculture, National Agricultural Statistics Services. *Livestock Slaughter.* 21 Dec 2012. Web. 1 Mar 2013. <http://usda01.library.cornell.edu/usda/nass/LiveSlau//2010s/2012/LiveSlau-12-21-2012.pdf>

———. *Poultry Slaughter 2011 Summary.* Feb 2012. Web. 1 Mar 2013. <http://usda01.library.cornell.edu/usda/nass/PoulSlauSu//2010s/2012/PoulSlauSu-02-24-2012.pdf>

———. *U.S. Broiler Industry Structure.* 27 Nov 2002. Web. 1 Mar 2013. <http://usda01.library.cornell.edu/usda/nass/industry-structure/specpo02.pdf>

United States Department of Agriculture. "USDA Data on Meat Consumption by Demographic." 2012. *Microsoft Excel* file.

United States Environmental Protection Agency. *Estimated Per Capita Fish Consumption in the United States.* U.S. EPA, Aug 2002. Web. 1 Mar 2013. <http://water.epa.gov/scitech/swguidance/standards/criteria/health/upload/consumption_report.pdf>

"USA: Research Suggest 98% of Americans are Meat Eaters." *Humane Research Council.* 2007. 1 Mar 2013. <http://www.humanespot.org/content/usa-research-suggest-98-americans-are-meat-eaters>

Vanhonacker, F., Van Loo, E. J., Gellynck, X., and W. Verbeke. "Flemish Consumer Attitudes Toward More Sustainable Food Choices." *Appetite* 62 (2013):7–16.

"Vegan Outreach." Vegan Outreach. 2013. 1 Mar 2013. <http://www.veganoutreach.org>

"Vegetarian and Vegetarian Aware Shoppers." *Humane Research Council.* 2006. 1 Mar 2013. <http://www.humanespot.org/content/vegetarian-and-vegetarian-aware-shoppers>

"Vegetarian Foods—U.S." *Humane Research Council.* 2007. 1 Mar 2013. <http://www.humanespot.org/content/vegetarian-foods-us#more2244>

"Vegetarian Foods 2012 Executive Summary." *Key Note.* 2013. 1 Mar 2013. <http://www.keynote.co.uk/market-intelligence/view/product/10573/vegetarian-foodspy>

"Vegetarianism by Country." Wikipedia. 2013. 1 Mar 2013. <http://en.wikipedia.org/wiki/Vegetarianism_by_country>

"Vegetarians Around the World." European Vegetarian and Animal News Alliance. 4 Jan 2013. 1 Mar 2013. <http://www.evana.org/index.php?id=70650>

"VegFund Video Survey Results Final Report October 2012." *Humane Research Council.* Oct 2012. Web. 1 Mar 2013. <http://www.vegfund.org/blog/wp-content/uploads/VegFund-Video-Survey-Results-Final-Report-October-2012.pdf>

"Veggie Tales." *Humane Research Council.* 2006. 1 Mar 2013. <http://www.humanespot.org/content/veggie-tales>

"VegSocUK Information Sheet." *Vegetarian Society of the UK.* n.d. 1 Mar 2013. <http://www.artofhacking.com/IET/HEALTH/live/aoh_stats.htm>

Verbeke, W., and I. Vackier. "Individual Determinants of Fish Consumption: Application of the Theory of Planned Behavior." *Appetite* 44 (2005):67–82.

Viegas, J. "Eating Tofu Could Improve Your Sex Life." *Discovery*. 20 Nov 2012. 1 Mar 2013. <http://news.discovery.com/human/health/eating-tofu-could-improve-your-sex-life-121120.htm>

Vinnari, M. "The Past, Present and Future of Eating Meat in Finland." Turku: Uniprint, 2010.

Vinnari, M., Montonen, J., Harkanen, T., and S. Mannisto. "Identifying Vegetarians and their Food Consumption According to Self-Identification and Operationalized Definition in Finland." *Public Health Nutrition* 12.4 (2008):481–488.

Vollum, S., Buffington-Vollum, J., and D. R. Longmire. "Moral Disengagement and Attitudes About Violence Toward Animals." *Society & Animals* 12.3 (2004):209–235.

Walsh, R. "Lifestyle and Mental Health." *American Psychologist* 66.7 (2011):579–592.

Wang, Y., Beydoun, M. A., Caballero, B., Gary, T. L., and R. Lawrence. "Trends and Correlates in Meat Consumption Patterns in the U.S. Adult Population." *Public Health Nutrition* 13.9 (2010):1333–1345.

Wansink, B., "Overcoming the Taste Stigma of Soy." *Journal of Food Science* 68.8 (2003):2604–2606.

Wansink, B., and N. Chan. "Relation of Soy Consumption to Nutritional Knowledge." *Journal of Medicinal Food* 4.3 (2001):145–150.

Wansink, B., and S. B. Park. "Sensory Suggestiveness and Labeling: Do Soy Labels Bias Taste?" *Journal of Sensory Studies* 17 (2002):483–491.

Wansink, B., Painter, J. M., and K. van Ittersum. "Descriptive Menu Labels Effect On Sales." Cornell Hotel and Restaurant Administration Quarterly 42 (2001):68–72.

Wansink, B., Park, S. B., Sonka, S., and M. Morganosky. "How Soy Labeling Influences Preference and Taste." *International Food and Agribusiness Management Review* 3 (2000):85–94.

Wansink, B., van Ittersum, K., and K. E. Painter. "How Diet and Health Labels Influence Taste and Satiation." *Journal of Food Science* 69.9 (2004):S340–S346.

Wansink, B., Westgren, R. E., and M. M. Cheney. "Hierarchy of Nutritional Knowledge that Relates to the Consumption of a Functional Food." *Nutrition* 21 (2005):264–268.

Wansink, Brian. "Changing Eating Habits on the Home Front: Lost Lessons from World War II Research." *Journal of Public Policy & Marketing* 21.1 (2002):90–99.

Wasserman, M. D., Chapman, C. A., Milton, K., Gogarten, J. F., Wittwer, D. J., and T. E. Ziegler. "Estrogenic Plant Consumption Predicts Red Colobus Monkey (Procolobus Rufomitratus) Hormonal State and Behavior." *Hormones and Behavior* 62 (2012):553–562.

Wemelsfelder, F., Hunter, A. E., Paul, E. S., and A. B. Lawrence. "Assessing Pig Body Language: Agreement and Consistency Between Pig Farmers, Veterinarians, and Animal Activists." *Journal of Animal Science* 90 (2012):3652–65.

Westbury, H. R., and D. L. Neumann. "Empathy-Related Responses to Moving Film Stimuli Depicting Human and Non-Human Animal Targets in Negative Circumstances." *Biological Psychology* 78 (2008):66–74.

White, K. and J. Peloza. "Self-Benefit Versus Other-Benefit Marketing Appeals: Their Effectiveness in Generating Charitable Support." *Journal of Marketing* 73 (2009):109–124.

White, R. F., Seymour, J., and E. Frank. "Vegetarianism Among U.S. Women Physicians." *Journal of the American Dietetic Association* 99.5 (1999):595–598.

"Why Do People Become Vegans/Vegetarians? Survey Says: All of the Above." *Health News*. 2011. 1 Mar 2013. <http://www.healthcanal.com/life-style-fitness/19971 -Why-people-become-vegansvegetarians-Survey-says-all-the-above.html>

Wilson, M. S., Weatherall, A., and C. Butler. "A Rhetorical Approach to Discussions about Health and Vegetarianism." *Journal of Health Psychology* 9.4 (2004):567–581.

Winter, D. "Meat, Globalization and World Hunger." *Humane Research Council*. 20 Nov 2012. 1 Mar 2013. <http://www.humanespot.org/content/meat -globalization-and-world-hunger>

Wolfers, J. "For Better Sex, You Probably Need More Than Correlation." *Freakonomics*. 11 Feb 2009. Web. 1 Mar 2013. <http://www.freakonomics.com/2009/02/11/ for-better-sex-you-probably-need-more-than-correlation/>

Wong, M. "Beliefs and Personality Traits: What Sets Vegetarians Apart from the Rest?" *Vegetarian Journal* 1 (2006). Web. <http://www.vrg.org/journal/vj2006issue1/ vj2006issue1beliefs.htm>

Worsley, A., and G. Skrzypiec. "Teenage Vegetarianism: Prevalence, Social and Cognitive Contexts." *Appetite* 30 (1998):151–170.

"Would You Date a Vegetarian? 30 Percent of Omnivores Wouldn't." *Ecorazzi*. 2 Aug 2012. 1 Mar 2013. <http://www.ecosalon.com/would-you-date-a-vegetarian-30-percent-of-omnivores-wouldnt/>

Wuensch, K. L., Jenkins, K. W., and G. M. Poteat. "Misanthropy, Idealism and Attitudes Toward Animals." *Anthrozoös* 15.2 (2002):139–149.

Wyker, B. A., and K. K. Davison. "Behavioral Change Theories Can Inform the Prediction of Young Adults' Adoption of a Plant-based Diet." *Society for Nutrition Education* 42.3 (2010):168–177.

Yasmin, H., and A. Mavuso. "A Study on the Meat and Vegetarianism Beliefs Among Swazis." *Nurture* 3 (2009):45–48.

York, R., and M. H. Gossard. "Cross-National Meat and Fish Consumption: Exploring the Effects of Modernization and Ecological Context." *Ecological Economics* 48 (2004):293–302.

ABOUT THE AUTHOR

 NICK COONEY is the founder of The Humane League, an animal advocacy organization based in Philadelphia, PA, that focuses on farm animal protection issues. He has written for publications including *The Philadelphia Inquirer* and *Z Magazine,* and his advocacy work has been featured in hundreds of media outlets including *Time,* the *Wall Street Journal,* and National Public Radio. Nick holds a degree in Non-Violence Studies from Hofstra University and formerly worked conducting nutrition education programs with the University of Pennsylvania's Urban Nutrition Initiative. He is also the author of *Change of Heart: What Psychology Can Teach Us About Spreading Social Change.* Please feel free to contact him at: nick.cooney@gmail.com.

ABOUT THE PUBLISHER

LANTERN BOOKS was founded in 1999 on the principle of living with a greater depth and commitment to the preservation of the natural world. In addition to publishing books on animal advocacy, vegetarianism, religion, and environmentalism, Lantern is dedicated to printing books in the U.S. on recycled paper and saving resources in day-to-day operations. Lantern is honored to be a recipient of the highest standard in environmentally responsible publishing from the Green Press Initiative.

www.lanternbooks.com